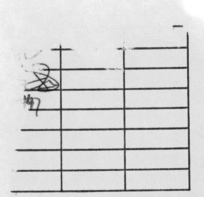

WESTERN AMERICAN WRITING
Tradition and Promise

CHAMPLAIN COLLEGE

WESTERN AMERICAN WRITING
～ Tradition and Promise ～

Jay Gurian

everett / edwards, inc.
post office box 1060 / deland, florida 32720

Library of Congress Cataloging in Publication Data

Gurian, Jay.
    Western American Writing: Tradition and Promise

    Bibliography: p.
    1. American literature — The West — History and criticism — Addresses, essays, lectures.
I. Title.
PS271.G87   810'.9   74-82195
ISBN 0-912112-04-2

To a new kind of Western — and American — Hero. The seeker after a new American dream, the defender of a new moral frontier.

Contents

Foreword
by Roderick Nash

This book constitutes evidence that Americans have finally become civilized enough to appreciate wildness. For much of the American experience it was all the other way; heroes *had* to be conquerors of wildness in both man and nature. Law, order, profit, progress and civilization were the venerated pillars of the establishment. These institutions and associated values constitute what Jay Gurian calls here the "Romance of Democratic Settlement." It permeated our individual and collective consciousness during an era when we lacked sufficient confidence to accord value to the antipode: Gurian's "Romance of Lawlessness." But given today's post-civilized anxieties we are as a culture at last ready to attempt a blending of the best of both worlds. The Western experience, Gurian tells us, is useful as a metaphorical vehicle for making the combination.

The quest for an optimum blend of civilization and wildness has lengthy roots in the United States. It is possible to find harbingers of the themes Gurian identifies in Western literature in the actual life and the myth of Andrew Jackson. John William Ward's *Andrew Jackson: Symbol for an Age* (1955) was among the first to notice how within a month, late in 1814 and early the following year, Jackson broke the power of both the South's most powerful Indian tribe and the cream of the British army. For his comtemporaries, Jackson's victories at Horseshoe Bend and New Orleans constituted evidence that the American was a new superman. As embodied in Jackson, the American occupied an optimum position on the spectrum of human conditions — midway between and better than both savagery and refinement.

Of course it was the frontier that permitted the American experiment, with the polarizing forces of Democratic Settlement and Lawlessness. The early American environment shaded off from the near-European conditions that pertained in Boston and Phildelphia to a wild West, and the occupants of that heterogeneous environment also tended to be complex combinations. There were options in America unknown to either the Indian or the Englishman. So Davy Crockett could, according to legend, kill a "b'ar" when he was only three, then return from the wilds of Tennessee to, in the words of the 1950s song, "patch up the crack in the Liberty Bell." Crockett, in Gurian's terms, was participating in both the Romance of Lawlessness and the Romance of Democratic Settlement. To take only the best known example, so was Theodore Roosevelt, whose career in government alternated with Western hunting and ranching, African safaris, and a mad dash up San Juan Hill. The Rough Riders of the last escapade, explains G. Edward White in *The Eastern Establishment and the Western Experience* (1968) were a symbolic combination of real Western cowboys and Eastern Ivy League athletes. In more philosophical moments Roosevelt analyzed the early 20th-century American as an increasingly "overcivilized man" in danger of losing "the great fighting, masterful virtues." Not for a moment did Roosevelt wish to return permanently to a savage, lawless condition; his goal was a careful mixture of wildness and civilization.

The preeminent American philosopher of the tension between the poles around which Gurian weaves his essays was, unquestionably, Henry David Thoreau. Although invariably discussed in the context of Eastern Transcendentalism, Thoreau could well be considered a Western writer and precursor to Gurian's subjects. Walden Pond may not have been Lake Tahoe, but for Thoreau, it was both literally and metaphorically the West. In going to Walden in 1845 Thoreau

sought "a border life." He explained that he "would not have
. . . every part of man cultivated, any more than . . . every acre
of earth." The ideal for both was *partial* cultivation. Ralph
Waldo Emerson helped Thoreau make the point when he
wrote: "In history the great moment is when the savage is just
ceasing to be a savage . . . Everything good is nature and the
world is in that moment of transition, when the swarthy juices
still flow plentifully from nature, but their astringency or
acridity is got out by ethics or humanity."

The problem with the human condition Emerson described
is that it is transitory. The savage "just ceasing to be a savage"
becomes civilized and, in time, overcivilized. As a nation,
America followed a similar route. The 1960s finally found a
sizeable part of American society prepared to question the
values of what was called the "Establishment." Jay Gurian
rightly sees the allegiances of the "counterculture" as tending
toward the wild, the natural, the Romance of Lawlessness.
Like Huckleberry Finn, the hippies of the 1960s had seen
enough of civilization and were ready to "light out" for
whatever unsettled territory remained. Like Nick Carroway
they stood at the end of Gatsby's pier and thought about the
totally uncivilized "fresh, green breast of the new world." But
this dream, Jay Gurian reminds us, should not be equated with
mere escapism. The ongoing challenge is to break the
intellectual strangleholds imposed by the two Romances, to
find new ways of mixing and combining. Western literature has
been and could be a palette for such blending. Implicit in this
book is the idea that, for the long-term well being of American
civilization, it had better be.

Roderick Nash
Santa Barbara, California

Preface

With the exception of "Style in the Literary Desert: Mary Austin," "The West and the New Dissent," and the Conclusion, these essays have been published as articles. Though written at different times and from a variety of perspectives, they relate to each other in ways which justify their appearance under one cover.

While a great deal of "western writing" is constantly published, there has been very little attempt to define a written tradition. Such a tradition would require thematic continuity across type. We would be able to find that western historians, novelists, poets, journalists, critics and scenarists have all created their work from the point of view of certain commonly held assumptions about the western reality, past and present. These assumptions would make up the "themes" on which a story line was developed or a chronological interpretation of past events was re-created. For example, if there were such a western tradition, then we should not be surprised to discover that Frederick Jackson Turner's interpretation of the meaning of the West in mid-nineteenth century America is evident in the manner of a western novelist like Frederick Manfred when he interplays characters in his plots.

Thematic continuity, in turn, provides one important basis for style. To conclude that there is a continuous tradition in western writing, we would have to be able to discover a series of stylistic consistencies across type. If a great many fiction writers over a long period of time have tended to elaborate their plots in the epic manner, then we would expect to find an "epic tendency" in the manner of historians re-creating the western past.

In the interplay of what may be called "the contradicting romances," I believe it is possible to discover a continuing and fundamental tradition which has had a crucial effect on western American writing of every type since the beginning of settlement. In the Introduction, I try to elaborate the value patterns and embodiments of these romances. The essays then investigate both this continuing basic tradition and the changes it is undergoing. In both his central thesis and its elaborations, Turner was more a romantic ideologist than an historian. He gave classic expression to a pattern of values that had dominated both popular and academic thought throughout the century that preceded him. He influenced a wide variety of western non-historical writers and was in turn influenced by them. Because of this connection I have included in the Appendix "Frederick Jackson Turner and the Contradicting Romances," a treatment of Turner's essentially mythic vision.

Within an ongoing tradition there are always counter-tendencies. These are based in the prevailing mode, yet are antagonistic to it. Thus, Mary Austin published a set of short stories in 1909 which expressed the same thematic approval of the "free individual" in an overwhelming natural world as that expressed by Turner, but she imposed on her materials a style not before used in the same context. This style was based upon understatement and aesthetic distance, strongly echoing the manner of Henry James. Generally, hyperbole and photographic realism are stylistic hallmarks of western story writers. Does change, or at least modification in theme and style mean the death of the old tradition, or merely its maturing? I hope these essays will contribute a little toward answering such questions.

Writers in all the fields discussed in the essays may be regarded as craftsmen using the same set of raw materials to create a variety of products. A history of mining settlement, for example, is inherently related to a piece of fiction set in the same experience. Precisely because our culture has developed a traditional way of relating the western past to the American past, writers of all kinds are closer to each other in theme and style than the formal distinctions between their crafts or disciplines would suggest. They need to be considered together.

JAY GURIAN

Acknowledgments

Written over a period of years in Minnesota, India, Wisconsin, Hawaii, Wyoming and Colorado, these chapters owe much to the clear-mindedness and devotion of my wife. Though her editing sometimes annoyed me, it invariably helped me say twice as much with only half as much pomposity.

My academic debts are more diffuse, though as real, beginning with the American Studies Ph.D. Seminar of 1961-62 at the University of Minnesota under Professor Charles H. Foster. Writing then about myths and fiction in conceptual terms, I began to search seriously for western American literary patterns. A summer grant from the McKnight Foundation of St. Paul made it possible to do field work in Wyoming and Nevada which partly resulted in the chapters on mining community literature. During that summer, Lola Homsher (now retired) and her staff at the Wyoming State Archives and Historical Department were extremely helpful. While I was exchange teaching at the University of Wyoming, 1970-71, the staff of the Western Historical Collection provided willing assistance for another book, some of which spilled into this book's latest chapters.

Novelist Thomas Berger was kind enough to correspond freely about *Little Big Man* and to permit my quoting him.

The following have appeared previously, and all the journals listed below have kindly consented to their reproduction:

"Sweetwater Journalism and Western Myth," *Annals of Wyoming*, April, 1964; "The Unwritten West," *The American West*, Winter, 1965; "Literary Convention and the Mining Romance," *Journal of the West*, January, 1966; "The Romantic Necessity in Literary Naturalism," *American Literature*, March, 1966; "The Possibility of a Western Poetics," *The Colorado Quarterly*, Summer, 1966; "Style in the Literary Desert: Little Big Man," *Western American Literature*, Spring, 1969.

"The West and the New Dissent" was first read at the Western History Association's annual conference, Omaha, 1969.

Introduction

Contradicting Romances in Western Writing

These essays are related by traditional assumptions about the meaning of the American West shared by writers of fiction, journalism, poetry and history. But the West is not the simple place of myth and tall tale most of them have pictured. It has always been much more complex than its written tradition implies. Historian Ray Billington recently said that it was "the nation's most complex region." We cannot even define its exact location. Today we say that the lands cut by the Rockies and the Sierras are "the West," but to Presidents and panhandlers the West of 150 years ago was far larger. It included the entire area of the Louisiana Purchase, the Northwest Territory (which began with Ohio), parts of what is now Canada and what was then Mexico.

In 1896, Frederick Jackson Turner, the most influential of western historians, called the West "a form of society, rather than an area." A Midwesterner himself, he saw America's settlement as a clash between European civilization and North American savagery. As we shall see, this is the view of John Locke, whose interest in America as an extension of Renaissance geography and ideology has been a powerful influence in the western American tradition. Turner saw that the point of impact between savagery and civilization was the frontier. Since the west-moving nation took its identity from this

1

impact, he called America a frontier society. Turner pushed the West back to Plymouth Rock, Jamestown and St. Augustine. Walter Prescott Webb, a later historian, went further. He pointed out that actually our own frontier was an extension of Europe's westward thrust. In an interpretation that would have made great sense to John Locke, Webb made Cortez, Henrik Hudson, Captain John Smith and Cartier kin to mountain men and cattlemen.

In 1688, John Locke wrote: "Thus in the beginning, all the world was America."[1] The insight climaxed his classic discussion of Property in the *Second Treatise on Government.* It accurately made metaphorical the place of the New World in the thinking of the late Renaissance. In this fabled environment, the natural laws of society and science would work out the many versions of natural rights which circulated among philosophers, statesmen and artists. Locke asserted that "the chief end" of civil society "is the preservation of property," including of course, real property, property for bodily subsistence, and the property of one's own body.

In the continuous tradition of Aristotle, Locke believed the ideal was to be achieved through a balance of property controlled by a balance of political power. Property began in labor, for "The labor of his body and the work of his hands we may say are properly his." But equally, the closer men are to a state of nature, the more likely that they will convert their desire for property to greed. "The same law of nature that does...give us property, does also bound [it]." In economic terms, greed is excess accumulation. How can "the industrious and rational" (Locke's European readers, involved in the settling of America) draw the line? The philosopher's formula was:

> As much as anyone can make use of to any advantage of life before it spoils, so much he may by his labour fix a property in; whatever is beyond this, is more than his share, and belongs to others. Nothing was made by God for man to spoil or destroy.

The communitarian goal of "the general good" implied by this rational yardstick was to be embodied in the western Romance of Democratic Settlement. It was to be made metaphorical by artist and historian alike in what Henry Nash Smith has called The Myth of the Garden. The hero of this agrarian utopia was the yeoman farmer.

But Locke's theories, like the western American tradition that grew partly out of them, involved a fundamental contradiction. He adamantly believed that though God "gave the world to men in common," He did not mean that it should remain so. God intended that "the industrious and rational" should transform nature into commodity. Three useful provisions of nature, the acorn, water and skins, were to be made into "more useful commodities," bread, drink and clothing. Industriousness achieved this transformation, thereby becoming a prime human virtue most clearly developed in an environment abundantly containing acorns, water and animals in the first place; that is, America.

In this scheme, the more industrious and rational must have a way of preserving property values in excess of personal need — and that leads to money. Isn't this kind of accumulating enterprise natural?

> For I ask, what would a man value ten thousand or a hundred thousand acres of excellent land, ready cultivated, and well stocked too with cattle, in the middle of the inland parts of America, where he had no hopes of commerce with other parts of the world, to draw money to him by the sale of the product?

Thus enterprise tends to become excess accumulation achieved through acquisition as value, and aggressiveness as behavior. This was indeed the program of western settlement. The contradiction that Locke failed to resolve lies in the necessity for conflict between communitarian and individualistic settlement. Theoretically and in practice, individualism has always tended to break down the very respect for legalized limits and codes of social behavior which Locke himself considered basic to any rightly governed and harmoniously functioning society. In other words, in his first view of property, Locke reflected the impulse toward unviolent, rational, legal and collective social control; while in his second view of property he reflected the violent, acquisitive impulse which, in the western American tradition, quickly came to be embodied in the Romance of Lawlessness.

A romance is an idealized version of human values and behavior that enhances reality. Romance differs from myth in being an attitude that gives shape, but has no shape itself. When Henry Nash Smith discusses the myth of the garden in *Virgin Land,* he is dealing with shape, texture, time and character. His definition of myth is simple: "an intellectual construction that fuses concept and emotion into an image." The traditional "Garden" of this American myth was the prairie West, a secular Eden kept by a yeoman Adam:

> The master symbol of the garden embraced a cluster of metaphors expressing fecundity, growth, increase, and blissful labor in the earth, all centering about the heroic figure of the idealized frontier farmer armed with that supreme agrarian weapon, the sacred plow.[2]

Smith and many others have shown that we think of this agrarian Adam as a combination of Puritan character and Tidewater theory. He was hardworking, honest, ambitious, godly, a son of New England. He was also a lover of the land and the small farm; a pillar of village life; a believer in the natural rights of man; a son of Jefferson. He was an ideal-child of the religious Reformation and the political Enlightenment.

In complex and sweeping ways like these, myth expresses social values. But behind the myths are the romantic attitudes which a society encourages about itself, usually against contradictory realities. Behind the Myth of the Garden there is the Romance of Democratic Settlement, which affirms that the "good" end — civilization, commerce, culture and church — was the guiding goal of the American settler. We have here a pictorialization of Locke's ideal society. No matter where he went, or how, the farmer, merchant, speculator, soldier, miner, missionary, cowboy, banker or gunman rode, crawled, walked or drove into destiny with a load of democratic values and institutions to plant, drill, survey and teach the next West. The new westerner was not self-interested, but value-interested; he did not take, he gave, and democracy burst from the ground by the following spring. This pious though aggressive romance came from Europe with the explorers, the churchmen and the plain immigrant.

Similarly, behind the myth of the Western Hero, there is the Romance of Lawlessness. The western hero is a complex myth-character classically portrayed by James Fenimore Cooper in the Leatherstocking series, and in all the "sons of Leatherstocking," as Smith calls the mountain men, scouts, cowboys, lawmen and gunmen who have entertained the American public. The Western Hero operates outside the accepted social order, but often protects it. Daniel Boone, an advance model for Leatherstocking, has been shown both fleeing civilization and clearing the way for its advance. With grand mythic permission, the western hero in today's paper-back, movie or television serial overrides law and order. To our immense satisfaction, Billy the Kid, a psychotic killer in real life, has become a hero of story and ballet. Jesse James has become a six-gun Robin Hood. In the special world of the Western Hero, lawlessness has become a virtue. In the Romance of Lawlessness, which stimulated the myth of the Western Hero, violations of law and disrespect for order were justified by the natural wealth, scanty "uncivilized" popula-tion, and the harsh physical demands of the many Wests. This romance suspends the Christian standards of right and wrong, and mocks the very institutions which are the justifications of the Romance of Democratic Settlement. While one romance glorifies violence, death, and "evil," in the various frontiers, the other glorifies peace, order, welfare and natural goodness. The romances contradict each other in the values they express. The contradiction is apparently reconciled by the necessity to use undemocratic and unchristian means to bring democracy and Christianity to the property which "industrious and rational men" must settle. The Western Hero is forever trampling down the yeoman Adam's garden; but that's all right, because when he takes the law into his own hands, he really has the good of the law in mind.

The effects of these romances have been so powerful that the entire nature of American development would have been different without them. We can analyze their terms in written history and printed story, but we must realize that they also existed as everyday forces in American thinking and acting. Presidents and Congresses, formulating national policy, have been influenced by these romances just as much as farmers, carpenters and store clerks. As he jockeyed the nation into the Mexican War, President Polk was no doubt able to justify himself through these contradictions. Many an elderly settler, looking back in speeches or written reminiscence to the early days of settlement, has assured the next generation of the rightness of killing, shooting, corruption and disorder. And the continuing ability of these romances to distort the writer's presentation of western settlement makes it clear that they are still the most powerful force in thinking about the West. When combined by Bernard DeVoto, a devoted western apologist, in a recipe heavily salted with literary style, they have an irresistible appeal:

> The frontier was American energy in its highest phase. Here [along the Comstock Lode] on the eastern slope of Sun Mountain it attained a final incandescence. The sulphurets of silver created an era at once unique and a consummation. Great wealth in hard rock and speculative stocks, the chaos of frontiersmen seeking it, the drama of their conflicts, the violence of their life, the spectacle of their pleasures, and above all, the rhythm of destiny shaping the national experience — there seems no reason to deplore this. It was the end and fulfillment of a process that had begun on a gaunt shingle where Plymouth woods met the December sea.[3]

"The rhythm of destiny shaping the national experience" apparently began to pulse with the Pilgrim landing, and reached its logical climax in a "chaos of frontiersmen." It would be impossible to devise a more attractive way of romanticizing western excesses. *This* lawless chaos, at least, was the ultimate expression of both religious and humanitarian values.

As we see in DeVoto, and as we shall see in many other

western writers, so long as the killing contradiction between Lawlessness and Democratic Settlement is accepted, over-simplification and distortion must result. Literary integrity becomes difficult and, in many cases impossible, because the doings of the western hero, though physically heroic, are intellectually, morally and socially crippled. Indeed, the western hero tends to become nothing more than a commercial extension of the drive for private property. Lacking a complex, abstract world view to begin with, western writers traditionally fail to develop the complexities and nuances of style necessary for the transformation of material into either scholarly or literary art.

Nevertheless, critics have been looking for a western literature for decades. In the 1920's, American Literature teacher Jay Hubbell claimed in the *Southwest Review* that the literary history of the frontier had not been written. In 1961, western poet-novelist-teacher John Williams asked, "Why has there not emerged a modern novelist of the first rank to deal adequately with the subject?"[4] In the same article, "The 'western': Definition of a Myth," Williams suggested that the answer is "a misunderstanding of the nature of the subject... and a misunderstanding of its implications." He showed that most western writers cynically exploit the western "myth," of simple Good and Evil forces opposing each other in a gigantic landscape: the settler vs. the Indian, the settler vs. the cattlemen, the sheriff vs. the gunslinger. The serious western writers, he said, try to write the myth from the epical, rather than the mythic, point of view.

John Williams is right in noting that such serious western writers as A.B. Guthrie, Jr., and Frederick Manfred fail to create western characters who seem humanly true or impor-tant. Boone Caudill, the mountain man in Guthrie's *The Big Sky,* performs epic feats of survival, yet we never feel anything about him. As Williams says, "the epic character tends to be one-dimensional, flat and not particularly distinguished by intellectual or moral powers. His virtues are the simple ones of physical courage and strength, singleness of purpose and blind endurance." This perfectly describes both Boone Caudill, and Hugh Glass, the mountain man in Frederick Manfred's *Lord Grizzly.*

By contrast, "the mythic character is designed to generalize the subject" of the inner quest. Myth is the most immediate of literatures; it gives us characters who are larger than we, but like us too. The myth gods of high and primitive religions alike are omnipotent and flawed, superhuman and weak-willed, moral and immoral, sensible and silly, epical and comical. But Boone Caudill, Hugh Glass, and most western fictional characters have little of that contradictory humanness so familiar to even the most extravagant myths. They are set too distantly in the big sky or the great mountains, like "Lord Grizzly" himself, who at one point has left his small party to hunt game, and barely survived a tremendous hand-to-claw encounter with a giant grizzly bear.

When Hugh Glass regains consciousness, gouged down to rib bone, flesh ripped deep and raw, he crawls to the nearby stream, drinks wildly, then turns on his back to let the water cleanse and loosen flesh from bear skin. "Presently he felt the minnows tickling him and nibbling at his crusts....'Water is medicine but the minnies'll leech me. Purify the blood.'" Wolves and turkey buzzards surround him, awaiting their turn at his flesh. Incredibly, Hugh Glass will soon begin a two-hundred-mile crawl, unable to walk (one leg broken), his body nearly beyond mortality. For eighty tight pages, Frederick Manfred will detail Glass's patents for survival as he elbows and shins his way over the Great Plains, nudged by another grizzly, flattened by a sand storm, eaten rotten by maggots. He will chase wolves off a dead buffalo calf and for three days eat that calf's raw flesh. He will eat live ants, suck cactus for water, fry mice, and so on and so on. In *Lord Grizzly,* Manfred has only redone a familiar western legend. He has presented unreality with intense realism. The reader wanting adventure which sounds like life, will praise the book. But whose life? And what realism?

Serious western writers like Frederick Manfred would

proclaim, "Hugh Glass's life," and "what really happened to him." They mistake realism for reality. The literary art uses realism, but not for the purpose of realism. If he is interested in "reality," the writer in our time must use what really happened a century ago, not as it really happened, but as his readers can make sense of it. A crucial weakness of serious western writers is that, ignoring the sense of their own time, they cannot make the necessary myth of earlier times. They assume that Hugh Glass's fight with a grizzly, or his super-human "crawl" back to Fort Kiowa will "reach" their readers. It will not, as art; it will only reach them as entertainment. The serious western writer creates an entertainment, but uses the techniques and the points of view of art. The result is stylelessness.

On the other hand, style results from recreating a new experience of believable, often "real" materials and it does the recreating job itself. In this sense it is the heart of the written art. But Manfred's readers can only identify with Hugh Glass physically when he suddenly wrenches his torn, pained body. This is not at all the same as identifying with Hugh Glass. During the three months of his crawl, Hugh Glass is obsessed with memories of Jim Bridger and Fitz, his younger companions. He believes they deserted him to die. His only purpose in fighting on, is apparently to avenge this desertion — for they have broken the code of the mountain man. Here are the beginnings of feelings and consequences which we, Manfred's readers, can understand. But the crawl itself, intensely physical, has no reference beyond itself. Glass's wounds heal, he becomes stronger, he survives — so what? In a great story, there will be something special, some abstraction at work as a moral force in a character's "real" actions. Of course, the real Hugh Glass probably felt no such moral force — but it is precisely his fictioneer's business to impose a moral force on a physical action, not to enshrine the physical action itself.

Pretty much repaired, the month after his return to Fort Kiowa he signs on as hunter aboard a keelboat heading north in the Missouri River. He decides to hunt meat for the crew,

and join them after they round the big bend. Is this really his
motive? The keelboat owner doesn't want Hugh to leave the
boat.

> "Hugh, what's got into you? You out to make more
> trouble?"
>
> "Booshway, it's December already, and the way I'll have to
> hump it to the mountains afore the big snows come will take
> the gristle off a painter's tail."
>
> "Hugh, you ain't ready for wear yet with that bum leg.
> Hugh, there's somethin' wrong with you. You act like you're
> out to get even with somebody. Or somethin'. Like the boys
> back at Ft. Kiowa said."
>
> Hugh hid his eyes. He watched the keelboat swerve around a
> bobbing sawyer in the moiling tan waters.

In this prelude to melodrama, Hugh hides his eyes twice;
Manfred has made clear emotion, promised a cosmic retribu-
tion. For what? The young Jim Bridger and the young Fitz
have apparently left him for dead — do we sense any complex
set of ideas at work? Mountain man honor, Hugh kept
repeating as he crawled. But since we see nothing more special
about Glass, the apotheosis of Mountain Man, than his
doggone will to dadblame survive, how are we supposed to
look on the coming prowl for revenge as more than a dumb,
driving "impulse?"

Like all western legendary heroes, Hugh Glass is a legend
without a meaning, a hero without an Ideal. In the effort to
write what we may call "epical realism," writers like Manfred
are only capable of addition — the addition of details. Art is
made by subtraction and abstraction, not by addition.

To see how a western writer can successfully convert stark
epic-type settings, plots, and characters into myth materials,
we can look at Jack Schaefer's *Shane.* It has become a minor
literary classic, and a movie classic because the author faces up
to the contradicting romances, and tries to resolve them. The
contradictions make complexity of idea and simplicity of style
possible. *Shane* is a shorter novel than either *The Big Sky* or
Lord Grizzly — in fact one of its virtues is its slender intensity.
We have a stock situation — a pioneer family whose hard-

earned security is threatened by lawless cattlemen land-grabbers and a psychotic gunman. *Shane* has also the apparently stock "good" gunman. All the familiar western characters are here — excepting the Indian. Yet *Shane's* secret, its intensity, derives from Schaefer's ability to express all this anew. *Shane* has, in a word, *style,* and its style derives from the mythic quality which Schaefer manages to generate.

It is important that *Shane* has two central male characters. Shane himself is from first word to last, an incarnation of the western hero myth. "He rode into our valley in the summer of '89....I saw him ride far down the road where it swung into the valley from the open plain beyond." Astride his horse, the lone rider arrives from a distance — an "open" distance "beyond." Though Bob, the "kid" narrator, "saw nothing remarkable about him at a distance," he did see "a pair of cowhands, loping past him, stop and stare after him with a curious intentness." Thus before Shane even arrives at the small spread (farm), he has taken on a special quality.

When he does arrive, Bob is first impressed by his clothes. He is a study in black and brown. In *Virgin Land* Henry Nash Smith noted that one of the first romantic attractions of the western hero was the clothes he "affected." It is therefore not surprising that Shane's clothes are "impressive." But it is interesting that these clothes are dark, not brilliant, and confined only to two related color tones. This particular toning down of the hero myth begins a pattern consistent throughout the novel. For example, Bob notes that "He was not much above medium height, almost slight in build. He would have looked frail alongside father's square, solid bulk." Wister's Virginian had been roughly six feet, while the dime novels of the last century had portrayed the western hero as unusually tall and broad.

Shane has strength, of course; as a western hero he must. But note that it is an internalized strength: "But even I could read the endurance in the line of that dark figure and the quiet power in its effortless, unthinking adjustment to every movement of the tired horse." And again: "He rode easily, relaxed in the saddle, leaning his weight lazily into the stirrups. Yet even in this easiness was a suggestion of tension. It was the easiness of a coiled spring, of a trap set."

Shane also has mystery, a myth quality significant to his role as the individualist of distant places and accomplishments. At the end of his first evening in the Starrett household Joe and Marian decide that his counterpoint between ease and tension is "mysterious." Marian says, "Yes, of course. Mysterious. But more than that. Dangerous." Joe Starrett answers, significantly, "But not to us, my dear." Thus by the end of the first chapter we have a heroic horserider. We also have an undersized hero whose clothes are dark, not brilliant, and most important of all, whose sympathy is with the farmer.

As contrast to Shane we have, sketchily in the first chapter, fully by the end of the second chapter, Starrett the farmer. Physically his contrast to Shane is absolute: he is of "square solid bulk." As for his character, appropriately enough it is first sketched in terms of his land. Bob says that the Starrett spread "was not much, if you were thinking in terms of size and scope. But what there was was good. You could trust father for that." Again appropriately, his character is next sketched in terms of his family. "Father was planning, when he could get around to it, to build mother the parlor she wanted." Then, when he introduces Bob to Shane, he does so affectionately: "This here is Robert MacPherson Starrett. Too much name for a boy. I make it Bob." A little later, when Starrett rhapsodizes about his small farm and few head of cattle, he becomes the perfect incarnation of the early yeoman that Crevecouer had pictured in "What Is An American?": "Listen to me, Shane. The thing to do is pick your spot, get your land, your own land. Put in enough crops to carry you and make your money play with a small herd, not all horns and bone, but bred for meat and fenced in tight and fed right." Starrett goes on to say that the days of the great cattle herds are over and small farms (presumably with towns nearby resembling the "cluster of frame buildings" in this story) are going to be shaped out of the grazelands. He is picturing here the typical genesis of the rural western community.

The interesting thing is that Starrett's dream attracts Shane personally. He says: "Well now, that's mighty interesting. I've been hearing the same quite a lot lately, and from men with pretty clear heads. Maybe there's something to it." Then, as if to emphasize the horserider's acceptance of the civilizing process, Schaefer has Shane, who rode in with his gun off, keep it hidden in his saddle blanket.

However perfectly Starrett fits the yeoman ideal, he is also portrayed as something more than simply that ideal. Shane himself sounds the note that raises Joe somewhat toward the level of myth hero. When speaking to the other settlers about the cattle owner Fletcher's attempts to intimidate them, he says:

> Fletcher won't bother with the likes of you now. He's going to the limit and he knows the game....Now he'll head straight for the one real man in this valley, the man who's held you here and will go on trying to hold you and keep for you what's yours as long as there's life in him. He's standing between you and Fletcher and Wilson this minute and you ought to be thankful that once in a while this country turns out a man like Joe Starrett.

If Shane is from the beginning the real hero of the piece, he nevertheless shares his place. This sharing is obvious throughout, but most effectively symbolized I think in the long sequences in which together the two men conquer the old stump. Joe calls it "the one fool thing about this place I haven't licked yet." What Shane does, in effect, is share in the final act of civilizing the very kind of place which the hero of the western myth traditionally has fought to keep in a state of antisocial savagery. This turnabout, plus the fact that Shane and Starrett become brothers, (in the profoundest sense of "friendship,") indicates how close the two myths have come to each other. The friendship is deep, it stands the test of conflicts. The larger conflict is that between the cattleman and the farmer. The lesser conflict is that between the two heroes themselves, brought about by Marian's attraction for Shane.

When the first of these conflicts threatens to involve Shane to his possible destruction, Starrett decides to give up the farm he has struggled to build. Conversely, Shane is so stirred by this dream, and by his friendship for Joe, its main actor, that he decides at the crucial moment to give up the temporary peace and satisfaction he had found, and return to his habitual role as gunman. He does so specifically and only to protect the land and the family of the land. Even the manner of his actions, once he has returned to that role, indicates the shift in the myth: he asserts his strength quietly and reluctantly.

Judging from the continual interplay between what Shane wants to do and what his feeling of honor and dedication for the family and land (i.e., community) forces him to do, I read his story as the story of the western hero turning social and therefore in search of limited society. Something in Shane's experience has left him with a desire for belongingness. It would be ludicrous to carry this interpretation too far. Nevertheless, there is a folksy but definite element of dramatic irony in the playing out of circumstances that force the gunman who finds peace and substance in the land, to give these up and return to violence and isolation in order to protect the land and its people. He performs the role of a hero in this — he is sacrificial, unconquerable and practically omniscient, but no longer the simple western hero, for he is troubled. If Shane does stand for the western hero in the public culture, as is indicated by his popularity and acceptance, then he has been taken with a grain of the confusion between individualist and "togetherness" drives that exist in that culture.

The other conflict between Shane and Starrett also symbolizes the shifting terms of the myths which they represent. Shane, as a western hero is of course attractive to women, and Marian, the only woman in the story, promptly falls for him. Unlike the rampaging variation of the western hero who conventionally is portrayed as dividing his pleasures between gun play and bed play,[5] Shane responds to Marian's emotion without exacting his pound of flesh. And unlike the

Platonic version of the western hero, exemplified by the Lone Ranger, he does not ride up the trail at the earliest suspicion that he is desired. Very humanly, Shane worries about the mutual attraction and decides that he had better leave. This is not his only reason for deciding to leave, but Schaefer manages to make it seem a real one. Marian stops him.

> "And you've been thinking that maybe you'll be moving on."
>
> "And how did you know that?"
>
> "Because it's what you ought to do. For your own sake. But I'm asking you not to....Don't go, Shane. Joe needs you. More than ever now. More than he would ever say."
>
> "And you?" Shane's lips barely moved, and I was not sure of the words.
>
> Mother hesitated. Then her head went up. "Yes. It's only fair to say it. I need you too."

Schaefer also manages to make the reader believe that Shane's decision to stay is based on Starrett's, not Marian's, need for him. The lines of the love triangle are sketched by Shane's respect for Starrett, and family, and by Marian's emotional confusion. This confusion revolves as much around what each man represents, as around each man *per se*. She is very effectively shown in this turmoil after the saloon brawl, when she tends her husband's and Shane's wounds at the same time:

> Her voice was climbing and she was looking back and forth and losing control of herself. "Did ever a woman have two such men?" And she turned from them and reached out blindly for a chair and sank into it and dropped her face into her hands and the tears came.

Both men were aware of each other's awareness of Marian's attraction for Shane, as the boy says: "The two stared at her and then at each other in that adult knowledge beyond my understanding." Now Starrett accepts Shane's effect on Marian with unbelievable grace, but in his acceptance there is a significant statement: "Don't fret yourself, Marian. I'm man enough to know a better when his trail meets mine. Whatever happens will be allright." There are two important points here.

First, Joe's fatalism, believable or not, is in the mythic rather than the realistic tradition, for here he displays superhuman (i.e., heroic) self-confidence. I mean that he is able to react without jealousy, and to keep faith in his masculinity while admitting that it has been topped. Second, Shane remains to the end the real hero: Joe can accept him as "better," feeling intuitively that there are no ultimate grounds for competition.

There is a danger, obviously, of reading too much into *Shane;* it is hardly even a novel, more a folk tale written in popular form. Its details are realistic but its central characters and situations, though believable, are both idealized. It retains many of the cliches of the separate Romances and myths: the inevitable barroom brawl, the shooting match (which the hero always wins after suffering a flesh wound), the two-gun badman, the tireless, ax-wielding pioneer, and so on. But along with these simplifications and cliches *Shane* contains, as we have seen, two complicated patterns which, in the working out of the plot, amount to a running together of the yeoman pioneer and western gunman hero myths. The result is a new pattern, one that is not accidental: it is not a fortuitous collection of new plot and character lines on the part of a single writer. Schaefer seems to have set about to do something new with worn materials, by writing in the mythic manner.

The mythic manner, in turn, embodies the content of the contradicting romances. We are forced to think about and to feel the contrary impulses of lawlessness and democratic settlement. We are forced to sense that the contradiction is inherent in the human species, as it was inherent in Locke's attempt to philosophize human existence. In this sense we may say that all western writing which hopes to rise above the level of entertainment must begin with an attempt to present the contradictory nature of the two romances. The western hero and the western yeoman must be juxtaposed, but not merely in narrative conflict. The antagonistic impulses which they represent must be mythicized. Further, the form of the mythicization, as well as its style, must be such that contemporary readers can identify their own conceptions with the past from which they have been derived. The western past requires what we may call an "aesthetic politics," a manner of re-creation which will make it possible for Americans to interpret the western past in terms of abstract values. Traditionally, the only value encouraged by our view of the West has been patriotic. As we shall see in the following essays, historians and novelists, journalists and poets have tended to play upon their readers' emotions, with the help of a romantic point of view, so that energy, resourcefulness, courage, enterprise and adventure all seem to take on meaning *because* men were settling the land for the glory of the new nation.

Patriotism is the most glaring oversimplification to which the contradicting romances lead; and violence is the most powerful distortion. This distortion is a purposeful (often unconscious) selection of events, sources, symbols, diction and point of view to dramatize the Romances. As in *Lord Grizzly*, or in Turner's "Significance of the Frontier," it has the effect of exaggerating one dimension of the past by blanking out others. If it is true that violence is a strangely attractive factor in prevailing middle-class American values, then probably its exaggeration in the western American tradition is largely responsible.

The problem in both American society and the western tradition is not that so much violence is dramatized, but that violence has been so thoroughly distorted into positive value. There is a crucial connection between the manner in which a western historian glorifies gunplay, and the way his son drives through a speed-restricted zone. The violence of world war or a Plains War may be presented with utterly graphic realism, yet in a value frame which will make it seem repugnant, or attractive − or most likely, both. But if the Romance of Lawlessness causes the actual violence of western settlement to seem *only* attractive, then it becomes a powerful force in socializing violence. Though such distortion and oversimplification are traditional, they have been challenged on a broad front in recent western writing, and as we shall see, occasional-

Literary Convention and the
Mining Romance

Though histories of the American West bulge with excerpts from diaries, memoirs, letters, newspapers, travel books, pamphlets, government reports, magazines and regional portraits, historians have ignored the literary conventions that helped shape "the authentic picture" these sources are supposed to give. Even worse, they themselves have adopted many of the romantic excesses their sources practiced a century ago. These are two of the many lapses in method that result from romantic complacency.

As might be expected, in mining settlement history the effect of literary convention is even harder to measure in the amateur texts of immigrants, self-appointed journalists and government officials than in those of professionals. But such analysis is important. Contemporary traditions affected not only how accounts were written, but what was selected for the record. Arthur Schlesinger's description of the "new reading public" before the Civil War indicates one aspect of these traditions:

> The chief characteristic of the new reading public was the fact that it was only semi-literate, half-educated...it remained true that a writer who wished to appeal to a wide audience, thus garnering both profits and a reputation, must adapt this manner and matter to the tastes and intellectual capacity of a people whose book education had, for the most part, not gone beyond the level of the second or third grade. Such a public gazed with

childlike wonder at the world that lived on the printed page, and asked of it only that it should not violate those homely precepts of moral worth which formed a part of their religious lore. They demanded Christ-like heroes and heroines and satanic villains; they gagged at subtleties; and the poverty of their cultural experience made them place a premium on the sentimental and the romantic and on tales of adventure.[1]

Public tastes and education had an important effect on the images, details and vocabulary of mining chroniclers. Their style must be understood as distorting their content no matter how crude the style or how attractive the content.

In the historiography of the mining West, this simply is not done. Thus Ray Allen Billington neatly describes the emotions of abused, exhausted migrants as they arrived at the California gold fields:

However they came, the miseries of overland travel were forgotten as soon as they reached the mining country. "It seemed," one recorded in that ecstatic moment of arrival, "that every rock had a yellow tinge, and even our camp kettle, that I had thought in the morning the most filthy one I had ever seen, now appeared to be gilded — and I thought with more than one coat. During the night, yellow was the prevailing color in my dreams." Tired as they were, none thought of resting. Instead they scattered through the mines....With washing pan in hand, and with feverish gleams in their eyes, they set out to reap the fortunes that the guidebooks told them were there.[2]

This description in *The Far-Western Frontier* is much too neat. The historian has not weighed earnestly recollected facts against stylistic hyperbole. Rather, by using the quotation without comment (a tradition in mining commentary) he has implied its total accuracy. He has adopted the literary conventions of his source as his own: "Tired as they were, none thought of resting....With washing pan in hand, and with feverish gleams in their eyes...." Both in selection and compression of detail the effect is impressionistic. The "characters" the historian creates today are as romantic as their counterparts in magazines and travelbooks of a century ago.

I have purposely chosen one of the West's finest historians to emphasize this kind of distortion, based on the chief conventions in popular literature at the time of settlement: piety and melodrama. The paradox of this combination led in turn to burlesque, and accounts in part for Mark Twain's ability to satirize Nineteenth Century morals and manners.

The paradox was at work in historians then, as now. In *The Writing of American History,* Michael Kraus remarks that George Bancroft's "lack of objectivity" resulted partly from his writing "when history was something more than investigation into the past — it was supposed to give instruction." It is significant that Bancroft read Gibbon daily.[3] In fulfilling an important requisite of popular literature, Bancroft himself became part of the literature. His successful mixture of morality and adventure — of piety and melodrama — fit the leveling intellectual and religious trends of the time, and the Federal policies he supported. Again paradoxically, the pieties he supported were quite impious if judged by their Christian heritage. Democratic, Anglo-Saxon pieties were usually dramatized with bloody versions of the American Revolution, the excesses of Napoleon, and the violence of Americans who invaded foreign territories to kill the natives and squander the resources. This was the "official" view of the American past, present, and future.[4]

It is no wonder that the most written and read about figures in the first one-half of the last century were rapidly glamorized into naive attractive combinations of violence and order, the two Daniel Boones, as Henry Nash Smith calls them. Boone was the first in a long line of popular frontier heroes whose effects on popular thinking (hence literary convention) have been too varied to measure. In the "official" view, Boone was a "standard bearer of civilization and refinement," defending the divine right to clear the wilderness for his enlightened society. But in the "popular" view, the half-savage Boone fled from society to protect that same wild nature with its dramatic conflicts, murderous demands and awful catastrophes. This contradictory western heroism continues to please mass tastes today in entertainment, of course, but also in history books.[5]

If, as Smith says, Timothy Flint's immensely popular 1833 biography of Boone "embodies the prevalent confusion of attitudes," it is not surprising that popular literature also reflected both a hunger for savage melodrama and a thirst for moral rectitude.[6] The literature of the nineteenth century, and particularly the American nineteenth century, is the extreme of the curious enlightenment fallacy that evil can be rationalized. Mining settlement lawlessness is still presented not merely as social or legal fact, but as positive value. William B. Gillis, a Nevada friend of Mark Twain, published a charming example of this shallow notion called *Gold Rush Days with Mark Twain*. Following tradition, he selected only evidence to romanticize lawlessness, as when he said of Virginia City's criminals that,

> It would be an injustice to these men to class them as criminals in the common acceptance of the word. Most of them were good citizens in every way except in the matter of gun play. They were a free-hearted, fun-loving lot of fellows, ever ready to help where help was needed, and to generously contribute to everything that stood for the public good, but they were all "gun-men," quick to resent an insult or to avenge a wrong with a bullet.[7]

Out of context this may seem a facetious comment, but it was clearly intended as historical common sense. In his "Introduction" to Gillis's work, Cyril Clemens assures the reader that though the author was ninety years old at the time,

> The passing years have not dimmed the memory of Mr. Gillis. When he speaks of his friendship with Mark Twain we can rely upon what he tells us. It is fortunate for all lovers of Mark Twain that when those who knew him in his early mining days in the West have almost left us, we have these crisp, fresh, fascinating recollections of one who knew him as a fellow-miner in those romantic days of the after-glow of the great California gold rush.[8]

Again traditionally, Clemens is assuming total accuracy when convention, habit and old age would have made it impossible.

Actually, the popular literary demand for vigorous, brutalized heroes did not develop because Washington, Boone, Jackson, Kit Carson, or gunslinger Sam Brown were vigorous or brutal. In the first place it developed because the dominant English literary conventions during that time suited American requirements. Violent melodrama, lurid landscapes, blood-soaked intrigues had been popularized by the Gothics and perfected — with realistic and historical detail — by Sir Walter Scott. Dickens had up-dated melodrama, sentimentality and realism by urbanizing and burlesquing them. Framing their sensationalism in Christian doctrine, both writers dominated large reading publics. This is certainly not all they did. Dickens especially was capable of subtle characterization and complex theme, but this was their effect on literary convention. In a very real way Scott and Dickens influenced not only mining settlement literature, but the literature of the entire western movement. Future mining authors like Charles Shinn, Bret Harte and Dan DeQuille, and the legion of non-professionals, learned in school and in their adult reading that narrative required first of all exaggeration. In *The Anatomy of American Popular Culture,* Carl Bode says that "The 'forties grew up on Scott." He proves this with such popular writers as George Lippard, Timothy S. Arthur (*Ten Nights in a Bar-Room*), Joseph Ingraham, Susan Warner, Caroline Hentz and Harriet Beecher Stowe. In the literature of the mining settlement, as in these, excess is virtue.[9]

This stylized hyperbole may be seen in non-fiction guises on the non-professional level, and the basic similarities emphasize the universal practice. In 1870 Rossiter Raymond, U.S. Commissioner of Mining Statistics, published the composite *Statistics of Mines and Mining.*[10] This is an important document because it reports on all the mining states and territories and is written with a Jacksonian piety that tells a good deal about the "official" language that long survived Jackson, Clay and Benton. Regarding the recent, modest bonanza in the Sweetwater area of Territorial Wyoming, Raymond remarks:

> Indeed, the pioneers of Sweetwater may be proud of the
> result of their labors, and the whole country may rejoice and
> thank them for having reclaimed such a valuable portion of the
> vast wilderness of the great West to civilization and industry. In
> return, it becomes the duty of the government to protect these
> men in the future against further Indian outrages, and to extend
> freely such general aid to them as is consistent with the
> institutions and laws of a democratic republic.[11]

This is the vocabulary of democratic settlement, the pious,
high melodrama of the pioneer. The "pioneers of Sweetwater"
are saviors, "reclaiming" the vast wilderness as if it had once
been God's (and America's) but had lately fallen to evil
Indians and foreigners. Now the country may "rejoice," as for
heroes. To complete the plot of the political melodrama, "it
becomes the duty" of the Federal Government (*i.e.,* the
Army) to protect the divine land and its heroes from their
enemies.

Raymond's words, though conservative when compared to
those of practiced romancers, were not merely guided, but
dominated by the literary conventions I have been discussing.
One favorite phrase to express at once the West's grandiose
violence and its democratic pretensions was "vast wilderness."
This haunted noun and evocative adjective are a perfect
starting point for analyzing the diction of western romance.
They were part of a terminology familiar to the readers of
Timothy Flint, Thomas Hart Benton, James C. Fremont,
The Democratic Review, Walt Whitman and everyday settlement journalism. For instance, John W. Clampitt of the Salt
Lake City post office department automatically called on
romance when he wrote the postmaster general about the need
for an office in South Pass City, the leading Sweetwater
community:

> The population of South Pass City at one or two months
> from the present date will be at least three thousand, and
> judging from reports presumed to be reliable, by the 4th of July
> next, there will be a population of ten thousand persons to
> celebrate, at that point, the nation's anniversary. Miners,
> merchants, lawyers, physicians, sons of toil and the hardy

pioneers, who, amid storms and snow, and the wilds of unbroken nature, part the way to a civilization that reflects honor upon our race and land — are flocking thither. From the El Dorado upon the Pacific, the Sierras of Nevada, from Idaho and Montana, Utah and Colorado, they are "marching on" to Wyoming....Independent of wealth, the development of which forms in all cases for a people, the firmest foundation for permanent prosperity. I allude to agriculture. This section of country contains some of the finest and richest agricultural valleys to be found in this western country. The fertility of the soil is such, watered by pure mountain streams, that in a short period it will yield in return for the labors of the farmer, a rich harvest. [The "valleys" were the Wind River Valley region at the base of the Wind River Mountains, roughly 25 miles north of the mining area.] [12]

Neither the gold in the area nor the soil in the valleys nearby warranted the melodrama of his praise. Within two years Sweetwater was virtually abandoned as a mining possibility, and even after the Indians were "cleared out of it," the Wind River Valley remained a minor settlement stretch that has supported a town of only four thousand people. Clearly the "hardy pioneer" in the "wilds of unbroken nature" bringing "civilization that reflects honor upon our race and land" was only a variation on Gillis's "freehearted, fun-loving lot of fellows" whose gun-play in Virginia City must not be judged by conventional standards.

The influence of these literary conventions is clearest and most distorting in the writings of later historians who have professed to recreate in our time the "actuality" of mining settlement. The flashiest of these, Bernard DeVoto, has combined the principal ingredients in a way that no nineteenth century pamphleteer, historian or orator succeeded in doing so well. In *Mark Twain's America* he described Virginia City, Nevada as:

A noisy, violent, incredible city. Elsewhere in the West the miner labored in inaccessible gulches, and, for a bust, made infrequent pilgrimages to the big town....But there hard rock and the big town met in one continuous bust. The West consummated itself. When the shift ended, miners boiled out of the shafts, paused only to note the day's fluctuations on the ticker, and then diverted themselves in ways that were invented for them....As the Comstock climbed its blazing pathway, the barrooms became a Western art....Washoe drew sculptors on the grand tour to carve bawdy figures in ivory or marble toward whom the miner gestured his invitations. Painters down on their luck or merely alcoholic were washed inland from San Francisco....These were the accompaniment of a fine art, the plain song of American drinking, which first invaded Europe with our imaginative compounds.[13]

There is no need to italicize specific words or phrases, for the excesses of "individualistic" behavior emphasize themselves. The key to DeVoto's formula is the statement that "The West consummated itself." A few pages later, he tells us how:

The frontier was American energy in its highest phase. Here on the eastern slope of Sun Mountain it attained a final incandescence. The sulphurets of silver created an era at once unique and a consummation. Great wealth in hard rock and speculative stocks, the chaos of frontiersmen seeking it, the drama of their conflicts, the violence of their life, the spectacle of their pleasures, and above all, the rhythm of destiny shaping the national experience — there seems no reason to deplore this. It was the end and fulfillment of a process that had begun on a gaunt shingle where Plymouth woods met the December sea. It is perhaps time to stop regretting the behavior of molecular forces.[14]

"The rhythm of destiny shaping the national experience" apparently began to pulse with the Pilgrim landing and reached its logical climax in a "chaos of frontiersmen." It would be impossible to devise a more attractive way of romanticizing frontier excesses. This particular chaos, at least, was the ultimate of Democratic (*i.e.,* Christian) piety. DeVoto's terminology is similar to, but more imaginative than Post Office Agent Clampitt's, Mining Statistics Commissioner Raymond's, aging William Gillis's, and the words of Nevada's chief historian, Effie Mona Mack. Her *Mark Twain in Nevada* was published fifteen years after the DeVoto paean, but it pulses to the same rhythm:

All was excitement, avarice, lust, deviltry, and enterprise. A strange city, indeed, truly abounding in strange exhibitions and startling combinations of the human passions. Where on this earth was there ever such another place as Virginia City?[15]

"Enterprise" is conventionally — and tellingly — juxtaposed to the western excesses that are supposed to have been its rightful concommitants.

The irony of such literary history is that it is dominated by its subject. When Mark Twain described the Comstock in *The Territorial Enterprise, Roughing It* and newspapers all over the country, his purpose was to entertain and his basic method was burlesque. The purposes of DeVoto and Mack are to instruct, yet their use of literary conventions prevents them from doing so. Burlesque requires hyperbole, and in *Roughing It*, Twain provided plenty:

> Virginia had grown to be the "livest" town, for its age and population, that America had ever produced. The sidewalks swarmed with people — to such an extent, indeed, that it was generally no easy matter to stem the human tide....Joy sat on every countenance, and there was a glad, almost fierce, intensity in every eye, that told of the money-getting schemes that were seething in every brain and the high hope that held sway in every heart....It claimed a population of fifteen thousand to eighteen thousand, and all day long half of this little army swarmed the streets like bees and the other half swarmed among the drifts and tunnels of the "Comstock," hundreds of feet down....[16]

Twain is describing "Flush Times in Virginia City" without the piety that literary historians have since attached to the mining settlement. His graphic mixture of fact and hyperbole is appropriate and successful. The problem is not that Twain set the pattern by which Virginia City and its kind of settlement would be recorded and judged; the problem is that the Comstock's historians and Twain's critics have tacitly accepted the burlesque as the reality, the caricature as character. The copious details that dramatize alleged "reality" were selected to serve magazine and hardcover commerce. Isn't this for all practical purposes what western historians still do?

Even in the useful work of an avowed cultural historian we

can see the same dependence on older literary conventions.
When he describes "The Age of Gold" in *Culture on the
Moving Frontier*, Louis Wright tells us that,

> Gold seekers *swarmed* out from the East. The towns along
> the Mississippi filled with emigrants preparing to strike across
> the plains for the *golden West*. St. Louis...*swelled* in importance.
> Wagon trains lumbered across the plains and deserts *in an
> endless stream*....Ships from Europe, from Australia, and from
> the east and west coasts of South America, dropped passengers
> and cargo at San Francisco. These vessels frequently lost their
> crews who jumped ship and headed for the mines. Ships were
> reported riding at anchor *with only a cat aboard*. Everybody
> else had gone to the hills. (Italics added)[17]

When criticizing the methodology behind such writing one
feels apologetic, for when Wright uses anecdote as if it were
historical evidence, he is in distinguished company.

If there is any doubt that the lonely cat is anecdotal, this
passage may be compared with Bayard Taylor's description of
the "swarming" gold seekers at the California end of their
migration. As an already popular reconteur, it was natural that
Taylor write about the California settlement. *Eldorado*
appeared less than two years after the migrations began, and
was to play its definite part in shaping the style and content of
mining settlement writing.

> The story of 30,000 souls accomplishing a journey of more
> than 2,000 miles through a savage and but partially explored
> wilderness, crossing on their way two mountain chains equal to
> the Alps in height and asperity, besides broad tracts of burning
> desert, and plains of nearly equal desolation...has in it so much
> of heroism, of daring and of sublime endurance, that we may
> vainly question the records of any age for its equal. Standing as
> I was at the closing stage of that grand pilgrimage...it would be
> impossible to give...a complete idea of its many wonderful
> phases.[18]

Juxtaposed in the entire chapter from which I have quoted
is Taylor's recipe for the twin romances: *lawlessness* in the
familiar melodrama of Western nature, and *democratic settlement* in the equally familiar melodrama of individual heroics.

Unctuous piety flavors all. The "story of 30,000 souls" doubtless had in it "heroism of daring and sublime endurance," but it should be our business to question the nature of what was being dared and endured. By not approaching the "story" seriously, we have done disservice to the serious matter of understanding it.

More than one critic has seen that western settlement can no longer be formulated as its first writers and politicians wished it to be. Though Lewis Mumford has carefully cultivated his own romanticism, of "culture," he correctly begins a critique of the "Romanticism of the Pioneer" by connecting the phenomenon with Europe: "Pioneering may in part be described as the Romantic Movement in action." [19] Two of the movement's ingredients were heroic absurdity and sanctified ignorance. There is good reason to agree with Mumford that "The movement into backwoods America turned the European into a barbarian." [20] Mumford is also correct in reminding us that there was little if anything in mining or agricultural settlement to deserve the pieties of literary convention. "The vast gap between the hope of the Romantic Movement and the reality of the pioneer is one of the most sardonic jests in history." [21] More than one parallel can be found between Pioneering and the Crusades.

Yet official and popular pressures have forced history to retell the jest seriously, so that it appears to be precisely the pioneers who closed the gap between romantic "hope" and democratic reality. As long as the West's scholars continue to present history as politics and entertainment, there is little chance that we shall deeply understand an important part of the American past.

1.   In Norman Foerster *The Reinterpretation Of American Literature*, (New York, 1959), pp. 175-176.

2.   Ray Allen Billington, *The Far Western Frontier*, 1830-1860. (New York, 1956), p. 232.

3. Michael Kraus, *The Writing of American History,* (Norman, 1953), p. 123.

4. Merle Curti, *Probing Our Past.* "Dime Novels and the American Tradition," (New York, 1955); Louis Wright, *Culture On The Moving Frontier,* "Spiritual Agencies and Secular Agencies," (Bloomington, 1955).

5. Henry Nash Smith, *Virgin Land,* (New York, 1957), Chapter 5.

6. *Ibid.,* p. 59.

7. William B. Gillis, *Gold Rush Days With Mark Twain,* (New York, 1930), pp. 82-83.

8. *Ibid.,* p. xii.

9. Carl Bode, *The Anatomy Of American Popular Culture,* 1840-1861, (Berkeley, 1959), p. 150 and chapters 11 and 12.

10. There were also prior and subsequent yearly editions.

11. Rossiter Raymond. *Statistics Of Mines And Mining,* Executive Document No. 207, House of Representatives, 1869-1870. (Washington, 1870), p. 338.

12. "The Sweetwater Mines," March 28, 1868, Bancroft Library, Berkeley.

13. Bernard DeVoto, *Mark Twain's America,* Boston, 1932, pp. 123-124.

14. *Ibid.,* pp. 132-133.

15. Effie Mona Mack, *Mark Twain In Nevada,* (New York, 1947), p. 183.

16. Mark Twain, *Roughing It,* (New York, 1872), Vol. II, pp. 12-13.

17. Louis Wright, *Culture on the Moving Frontier* (Bloomington, 1955), p. 126.

18. Bayard Taylor, *Eldorado,* "The Overland Emigration of 1849," (New York, 1850).

19. Lewis Mumford, *The Golden Day,* (New York, 1926), p. 47.

20. *Ibid.,* p. 58.

21. *Ibid.,* p. 79.

Sweetwater Journalism and
Western Myth

Classically the frontier newspaper is described as a running chronicle of tall tales, lawlessness yarns and folk humor. *The Territorial Enterprise* of Virginia City, Nevada is often cited as the archetype of such hyperbole. Its columns bulged with "eye-witness accounts" of shootings, miners' violence, tainted women, barroom brawls, abused law officers, runaway men — and animals. These are supposed by such critics as Bernard DeVoto to have reflected the "reality" of western settlement.[1]

Little has been written to contradict or at least modify this over-generalization. Yet the three dozen surviving issues of South Pass City's two newspapers offer strong counter-evidence. They represent a sizable body of frontier journalism, contemporary with *The Enterprise*, that reflected and encouraged orderly, constructive communities. After all, there were scores of lesser mining community journals like *The Sweetwater Mines* for every sensational sheet like *The Enterprise* or *The Helena Gazette*. As the example of Sweetwater journalism shows, all of these need analysis before the DeVoto kind of generalization can be believed.

Who does know what went on in Virginia City, Nevada, or South Pass City, Wyoming, a hundred years ago? And what is really known? With investigation perfected by computer, caliper and seismograph, why haven't we had a revised version of bonanza since Mark Twain parodied gold rush days for eastern magazines? The entertainment market has kept a constant pressure on historical tradition, and American sentimentality about its frontier has kept a constant, intense pressure on entertainment. No one wants to give up the simple picture, for it provides handy heroes and exciting heroics. If you were putting together a survey text for high schools, would a publisher offer you a contract when you wrote that most mining towns were set up and run by sober, solid, middle-class citizens no more crooked or "sinful" than your neighbors? Would your son like to learn that most mining town dwellers got no closer to six-guns than to keep one in their storage chests for self-protection?

But there is just enough truth in the fairy tale version to make accuracy seem irrelevant. Both the Comstock and the Sweetwater began in the 1860's. Virginia City and Gold Hill were active Nevada communities for nearly thirty years; but the Sweetwater towns of South Pass City and Atlantic City, in central mountain Wyoming, were active only for three. The Comstock communities had between twenty and forty thousand people at various times. There were never more than two thousand in the Sweetwater area. Deep shaft mining prevailed at Comstock, but only surface and shallow-draft mining in Sweetwater. H.H. Bancroft, who ran a team of writers and turned out a vast history of the West, filled seventy pages with Comstock but only three with Sweetwater.

The Comstock bonanza is the most written about, the most sensationalized occurrence in western mining history. It competes with Custer's Last Stand, the Oklahoma land runs and the Johnson County War as ultimate western romance. During the 1850's, while the eastern slopes of the Sierras were still part of Indian country (according to regional tribes) and Mormon country (according to Brigham Young), occasional prospectors found surface gold and silver ore there. The word was passed along, and as many of the diggings in California gave out, prospecting to the north, south and east of Sonora country increased. The exact moment when the Comstock Lode was discovered to be rich is surrounded by legends which need not be recounted here; but in 1859 a "rush" to the high slopes crowned by Sun Mountain, began in earnest. By 1861, Virginia City and Gold Hill were thickly populated communities, and both surface and depth mining, more and more subsidized by San Francisco money, were attracting laborers, engineers, merchants, artisans and speculators of all kinds by the thousands.

The Sweetwater bonanza was much smaller than the one at Comstock, though the quality of its historical presentation is no higher. Random prospectors found gold in paying quantities in the Wind River Mountains as early as 1865. Late in the summer of 1867 claims were first staked out in a twenty square mile area not far north of the South Pass cut made by the Oregon Trail through the mountains. South Pass City was informally laid out just before the site was abandoned for the winter. In April, 1868, the "rush" began. We still have copies of newspaper articles and advertisements from Salt Lake City, Cheyenne and other towns along the Union Pacific Route, beckoning settlers to Sweetwater by glorifying the natural wealth there. At an altitude of nearly 8,000 feet, the Sweetwater area was workable only half the year, but from May through October of 1868, 1869 and 1870, it was yielding enough paydirt to support a population that varied between 500 and 2000. By 1871 it had become clear that this was a surface bonanza, and its three communities drifted into ghost township. The most elaborate historical treatment of Sweetwater combines the contradicting romances attractively and naively. In *The Ghost Towns of Wyoming*, by Mary Lou Pence and Lola Homsher, we are told that:

> The year 1868, though full of danger, was on the whole highly prosperous and South Pass City took its place as one of the great gold camps of the country. Along the main street were such caravansaries as the Eclipse, the Pass, the City, the South Pass and the United States. The partakers of distilled liquids found open the doors of the '49er, the Keg, Fatty's Place, the Magnolia, the Elephant, the Occidental, Fritz' Place, Gilman's, Bright and Shakespeare and Furgeson's. Here cards and bottles were shuffled night and day.

That the village was prospering was evidenced by the length-
ening of the main drag. There was now a gun store, a shooting
gallery, a bowling alley, a beer garden, a wholesale liquor house
and a jewelry shop. There were fracases night and day over
claims, and many resorted to the rule of wits and pistols. From
all this four law firms built up quite a lucrative practice....Even
trusted Postmaster George Dickinson [sic] got into the mood of
things and by hook and crook defaulted on his government and
skipped for the South African diamond mines.[2]

The jaunty, punning tone convinces the reader that "fracases"
and fraud were the rule of the day in South Pass City.
Actually, the town was a good deal more orderly and less
colorful than the Romance of Lawlessness makes it out to
have been. Romance led the authors to list no mercantile
establishments on "the main drag," only those places that
would suggest lawlessness. In their Foreword, Pence and
Homsher even declared that lawlessness in Wyoming mining
communities was not mere lawlessness, but a conscious
democratic drive in the men who stood at the bars and bought
up the guns:

The ghost towns of Wyoming deserve an important place in the
recounting of the state's history. Our decadent villages flou-
rished and declined during one of the progressive advances of a
nation to widen its scope of achievement. But in retrospect their
stories are alive with pioneer vigor and virility. The men and
women who peopled these places came West with few worldly
goods, but greatly endowed with the characteristics needed for
the development of the frontier — pride of enterprise and a
spirit of adventure; and they were thrilled by the romance of
the far-flung Western country.

Lawlessness has become "vigor and virility" or "characteristics
needed for the development of the frontier," which, in its
mining phase, was "one of the progressive advances of a nation
to widen its scope and achievement." The interworking
romances have fused the pioneer character and the miner
character, yet the record left by Sweetwater journalists
contradicts this picture.

Contrary of the editorial policy of The Enterprise, the

policies of both Sweetwater papers were based on the premise
that South Pass City and Atlantic City were law-abiding. There
is sufficient surviving evidence in court dockets, County
Commissioners' Minutes and other sources to make the
premise credible. It is impossible to be sure how much the
difference between Comstock and Sweetwater editorial policies reflected divergent "community realities." But it is
possible to prove the editorial assumptions of *The Sweetwater
Mines* and *The South Pass News* by analyzing editorial
comment and column content.

Thirty-five issues of *The Mines* are known to exist,
thirty-four in the Bancroft Library and one in the Denver
Public Library. In *Pioneer Printing in Wyoming,* Douglas
McMurtrie has speculated that the paper was probably first
issued Saturday, February 15,1868. The first extant issue is
dated March 21, published at Fort Bridger, southwest of
Sweetwater.[3] In the April 5 issue the editors, J.E. Warren and
Charles J. Hazard note:

> To those of our friends in this vicinity wanting Job Printing
> done, we say, bring in your orders this week, for we remove our
> office to South Pass City next week, wind and weather
> permitting. ("Local Matters" column)

But the April 11 and April 15 issues were datelined "Fort
Bridger." The first surviving South Pass City issue is dated May
27 as are the following fourteen survivors, the last dated
August 8. The next extant issue was dated November 25 and
was published in Bryan City along the Union Pacific construction line. Presumably the egress of miners for railroad work
and the inaccessability of the Sweetwater dictated the move.[4]
The next surviving South Pass City issue of *The Mines* is
dated April 7, 1869; one for June 19 and another for July 14,
completes the surviving Sweetwater-published total. But what
we have is enough to judge the editors' intentions during the
two summers of greatest Sweetwater activity.

In the first extant Sweetwater issue (May 27, 1868) under
"Local Matters" the editors printed two refutations of items in
The Helena Gazette (Montana) and *The Reese River Reveille*

(Nevada). Both papers had reported shootings in the Sweet-water area. First, Warren and Hazard desire "to correct a statement...in the case of the shooting [of] Lovejoy by Ryan." A South Pass citizen, Mr. Hust, was accused in *The Gazette* of inciting the incident, but he "desires us to say that no difficulty occurred between him and Mr. Ryan, and that all the participation he had in the affair (for he was present) was only in the character of a pacificator."

In the second case the editors correct a letter "from a passenger to the Sweetwater Mining country, published in the *Reveille,* alleging a well-known citizen of Austin," James McCarthy, to have shot a companion. The editors claim "to have heard all the facts in the case and in justice to Mr. McCarthy we desire to say that his friends are as numerous as ever," that McCarthy in fact arranged the wounded man's care, and that the wounded "was alone to blame." Strangely, there is only one other local gunplay incident in the seventeen extant issues published at South Pass City.[5] The virtual absence of such reporting, extreme for any newspaper, suggests that the editors designed consciously an image of lawfulness for the new communities.

The sources of these two items — other western news-papers — reflect a continuing habit of editors Warren and Hazard to borrow: a habit universal among western settlement journals. In the May 27, 1868 issue alone, aside from the two instances of borrowing above, the editors printed an eleven line anecdote from *The Enterprise* ("Mark Twain Bricked"), an eleven line report from *The Salt Lake Reporter* of gold strikes in Utah; and on the first page, an excerpt entitled "The Beauties of Wyoming" from *The Frontier Index,* a paper printed at various construction points along the Union Pacific line. A half column on the same page is filled with an excerpt from *The Owyhee Avalanche,* May 9, called "Northern Pacific Railroad." Still another item, from *The Cheyenne Argus,* tells about an overturned coach on the Cheyenne-Denver route. Borrowing was, of course, the handiest means at the time for reporting news beyond the locale, the press bureaus not yet having been established.[6]

A number of items in the "Local Matters" columns of the May 27 issue discuss community conditions. Referring to the telegraph line then being run from points south up to South Pass City, the editors remark:

> The object of the expedition is accomplished. A.C. Bassett, Esq., has completed arrangements by which the telegraph line will be up and in working order within the next two or three days. Many of the citizens here have contributed liberally towards getting the line established, but they will be amply repaid by the advantages to be derived from it....

And just below:

> We are pleased to see the energy exhibited by the miners on Rock Creek in opening up their claims....A great deal of preparatory work is being done and done well. We speak whereof we know, being an old miner ourself.

Two items later:

> The Board of County Commissioners will meet on Monday, June 1st, at ten o'clock A.M. at the office of the Register of Deeds.
>
> A.G. Turner
> Clerk of Board

The next item:

> Business men will not fail to read the notice in another column to all persons liable to pay license, and see if the "shoe" fits them.

In the next column the following appeared:

> NOTICE — Notice is hereby given to Merchants, Saloon Keepers, Butchers, and all persons liable to pay license, that unless they are paid by the 30th inst., that all unpaid will be put into the hands of the District Attorney for collection.
>
> H.A. Thompson
> Ex-Officio Treasurer

The same announcement appeared again in the next issue (May 30). The Minutes of the County Commissioners record that in their April 17, April 28, and May 11 meetings they had passed resolutions fixing license rates, as required in the statute that created Carter County. As further evidence of community organization it should be noted that the Commissioners did meet on June 1st, as announced.[7]

In a two-thirds column editorial in the same issue, titled "A Contrast," the editors take to task the get-rich-quick kind of miner:

> GROUPS OF SUCH UNFORTUNATES...can be seen assembled in the saloons and other public places, whiling away the time in telling stories of the lively times they have experienced in the different mining camps, or of the reputed wealth of some far off unexplored country....Well, this is one class that we come into contact with here, but fortunately they do not remain long to annoy anyone....However, we are thankful that, notwithstanding "all men are born free and equal," they differ in many respects, for we have another class of men here, who are quite the reverse of the one we have endeavored to describe who had [sic] not reared their air castles to such a giddy height before coming here, and who possessed sufficient energy and stamina to overcome the many obstacles found in their paths. Upon men of this kind do we depend for the future developments of this country, and we are confident that their effort will not cease until this object is accomplished....

The invocation of permanent settlement, hard work and diligence would not be significant except that it is so frequently echoed in the issues of *The Mines* that follow. It is the prevailing tone.

In the next issue, May 30, 1868, under "Local Matters," the editors recommend C.L. Lightburn's and John McGrather's "store," pointing out that Lightburn came to South Pass City in the winter of 1867 (just after its "laying out as a town") and remained through the winter "when business was dull, giving credit to many who needed goods, thus extending his former reputation for liberality in business matters...and by their upright and honorable dealings [the partners] have a well-deserved and an enviable reputation. We can recommend them." The partners, then, are valued for their cooperative, communitarian impulses.

The following item notes that William Rose and Edward

Gilman (California miners then at Sweetwater) considered the statements about Death Valley in the previous issue to have been exaggerated. Such correction of exaggeration is one of the editors' continual attempts to separate hyperbole from fact. The June 6 issue reports the "GRAND DEMOCRATIC MASS MEETING" that had been advertised in the June 3 issue. Despite the headline adjective, the report is straightforward. It begins by naming the time and place, the officers appointed to run the meeting, and the delegate chosen to represent Carter County at the National Convention. It continues, "The following motion was adopted, that a committee of three be appointed to draft resolutions expressive of the sentiments of the Democracy of this section...." It reports the names of the committee members chosen, reports adjournment, reconvention at 5 P.M., then gives in full the resolutions adopted. The last of these reads: "That the thanks of the meeting be tendered to the proprietors of the *Sweetwater Mines* for publishing the call for this meeting." In keeping with the general tone, the last paragraph of the article reports:

> The meeting was then addressed by J.M. Thurmond, Esq., Judge J.W. Stillman and Sheriff J.R. Murphy, after which cheers were given for the old Flag; much enthusiasm prevailed. The meeting adjourned at the call of the president.

The lack of flourish in this report is not unusual for Sweetwater journalism.

The rather sober tone already noted in a number of articles is reiterated in an excellent editorial for the June 10 issue. It somewhat duplicates the May 27 editorial on "steady settlers" already quoted. Its sentiments are so contrary in content and tone to what is allegedly "typical" of mining camp journalism, that they are worth noting at length:

> ### GO STEADY
>
> With the spring immigration come many to Sweetwater, who make their first advent into a mining country. They are some of them monied, some are merchants, many have only their labor for capital; but all have "great expectations." They are excited

by the tales of fabulous wealth buried here, buoyed up by the prospect of soon seeing huge bricks, great nuggets and splendid specimens, and for a time exist in a sensational, unnatural and unwholesome atmosphere, by which realities are sadly distorted. To all newcomers we say, "go steady." You who are poor go to work by the day, in gulch or mine, in store, or wherever you can find it. *Labor is no disgrace in Sweetwater.* In your woolen shirt and gum boots, other things being equal, you are a peer to the proudest. Be economical. You may earn $6 or $7 or $8 a day; more than a week's wages in the States; but don't squander it foolishly. There is not one "pilgrim" in fifty but that sees hard times the first winter....too many who do make money, yield to the allurements of the gaming table or the saloon, and are dead broke at the commencement of the long winter; you can make more money here than in the States; you have to contend strongly against the tendency it creates for extravagance and dissipation. You have much to learn before you are fitted for prospectors, or judging the value of mines....

The tone is neither pompous nor pious; it is rational. The editors rightly do not deny the presence of lawlessness and the distractions of "vice." It would be ridiculous to claim Sweetwater was as "settled in" as a New England community, but the significant point is, the editors do not romanticize anti-community behavior.

Only two pages remain of the July 18 issue, but the report therein of the Independence Day (July 4th) celebration is valuable as another expression of community value: "The day passed off quietly and orderly, not a single disturbance occurred in our streets, no accidents of any kind, although the firing of anvils, pistols, guns, etc., was kept up during the entire day." The writer goes on to praise the citizens' patriotism "Though far removed from our earlier homes on the western and eastern shores of our beloved country."

As previously pointed out, commentators emphasize that western newspapers were outlets for folk humor. Discussing a number of the more prominent Nineteenth Century newspaper humorists, Constance Rourke generalizes:

But their significance is chiefly that of their category, and one must persistently remember that they were only the more prominent of literally hundreds of humorists whose writing formed a great part of the material published in hundreds of newspapers all over America, and especially on the far-flung frontier.

The importance of this literature for history is its complete embodiment of frontier society.[8]

From the point of view of folk humor scholarship, newspaper humor can perhaps be defended as a "complete embodiment of frontier society," though as a generalization for western mining community history it must be questioned. "Humor" was never more than an incidental interest in Sweetwater journalism, as the following subject-matter breakdown of three scattered issues will show:

CONTENTS[9]	SM 5-27-68	SM 6-19-69	SPN 10-27-69
Advertisements	8½	12	8½
Local Affairs	4	3 1/3	3½
National and International News	3	1	6
Editorials	2/3	1½	0
Westernalia (nature, settlement, etc.)	1 1/3	0	0
Mining Laws, News, Data	2½	¼	½
General History	¼	3/5	0
Humor: Anecdote, Description, Editorial	3/5	1½	2/3
Territorial & Federal Government	0	0	4/5

The definition of humor that determined the figures above includes imported (borrowed) items, often from *The Territorial Enterprise,* and occasional attempts by Warren and Hazard or their writers. Though few, these suggest that folk humor was not the gift of every frontier newspaperman. One sample, worth citing because it deals with a favorite western subject, appeared in the June 10, 1868 issue:

> The great feature of the past week in South Pass City has been the opening of the magnificent Magnolia Saloon....George [Hust, proprietor] is known never to stop at trifles, when once he puts that broad shoulder of his to the wheel, *things* must move then or *bust*....All ye unwashed go to the Magnolia and take a look at yourselves in that magnificent $1,500 mirror behind the long refreshment stand, and our word for it, you'll feel a confounded sight better or worse, either one.

A squib in the May 30, 1868 issue is equally trite:

> We visited Atlantic City the other day, and were immediately seized by "Red Cloud," who carried us captive (as he was taken captive by that celebrated Indian Chief) to H.B. McComber's brewery and then and there dosed with the best ale we ever tasted in this Rocky Mountain Country. We owe "Red Cloud" one.

Three "tall tale" items can be found in surviving Sweetwater issues, of which the following is the longest. It was printed in *The Mines,* March 21, 1868, then being published at Fort Bridger. Under the title "Correspondence" the editors published a letter dated "March 14, Salt Lake City" and signed by "Hank Whip."

> Do you know, sir, that your little brick of a paper is sought here with as much avidity by both Mormon and Gentile, as a free lunch table would be by a corner loafer....Said a business man to me: "It contains more interesting reading matter than the Reese River Reveille...."

> The city is filled with strangers en route for the Sweetwater mines. The western coaches are coming in now loaded down with passengers for that destination....Whenever W.F. & Co. [Wells Fargo] stock the road between Fort Bridger and South Pass City as I understand they will shortly do — you may look for an influx of passengers whose number will require a daily dozen coaches to accommodate them. Already our hotels here are crowded with strangers from Austin, Virginia City, Gold Hill and elsewhere; and even San Francisco has her representatives here, bound for our new El Dorado. One of Dan DeQuill's pack trains is on the way here from Austin, Nevada, loaded with a general assortment of mining goods such as gum boots, quicksilver, etc....

> As this letter has already reached the full number of feet in length (3,000 ft.) allowed by the United States law on any one ledge, I must put my stake down and locate on something else in my next.

But exaggeration such as this, connecting Sweetwater with the principle bonanzas of Nevada and California, was never instituted in *The Mines.* Instead, Warren and Hazard chose to build up Sweetwater in terms of economic wealth that would bring prosperity and permanent settlement. This exaggeration clearly resembles the kind of western settlement oratory and writing which throws a quasi-religious mystique over the idea of "free land."[10] Miners and their families bound for Sweetwater are often referred to as "pilgrims for Sweetwater," or "the Sweetwater pilgrims." Besides themselves glorifying, the editors printed others' glorifications. In the March 28, 1868 issue they reprinted a long letter by John W. Clampitt, "Special Agent, Post Office Department," (Salt Lake City), outlining the proper posting procedure to and from Fort Bridger (where *The Mines* was still being published), and continuing with a copy of his own letter to the Postmaster General on the need for a post office at South Pass City. He expects that by next July Fourth the population will have reached 10,000.[11] A variety of professionals, toilers and pioneers who "part the way to a civilization that reflects honor upon our race and land" are on the way. Farmers have also set their sights on Sweetwater, which contains "some of the finest and richest agricultural valleys" in the entire West.[12]

While Clampitt's description is practically a parody of the "free land" exaggerations common during the Nineteenth Century, the editors' frequent local versions are on the whole notable for restraint. They seldom use trite phrases; they simply assume a wealth (though unproved till disproved) as part of the "gift of nature" American settlement must manifestly develop. Sometimes they are anecdotal, as in the May 27, 1868 issue:

> We have had brought to our notice a little circumstance that goes to show upon what slight foundation many men condemn a mining country. Two gentlemen, who came here a few days ago, concluded that there was no show for them and that they would leave for other parts, but while out hunting for their stock they discovered and located two ledges that they pronounced richer than anything they ever saw. The lodes are large and the rock exhibits free gold in abundance. These gentlemen are now of the opinion that the country abounds in rich ledges and that not one quarter of them have yet been

discovered, to which sensible opinion we must decidedly concur.

Sometimes the editors themselves defend Sweetwater's wealth. The June 6, 1868 editorial takes off at *The Helena Herald:*

> Notwithstanding the false reports and willful misrepresentations which have been circulating concerning our mines in this Sweetwater country, they fully come up to the expectations of all the sensible and experienced men who have come here....The *Herald,* a virile and insinuating sheet, but unfortunately devoid of influence...comes out again, its columns fraught with falsehoods as usual concerning this country....A short time since we saw a statement in the *Herald,* about the great number of people, who had taken their advice, and staid [sic] away from Sweetwater. This continuous boasting of the *Herald* about their unbounded *influence*....reminds us of the heroic deeds performed by SIR JOHN FALSTAFF, as stated by himself.

This is one of the few examples of inter-journal mudslinging to be found in the surviving issues of *The Mines.* In their July 3, 1868 issue the editors more mildly report the arrival of three wagon teams "loaded with provisions" from Salt Lake City:

> We hope, ere long, to see both the demand and supply increased in our vicinity, and without doubt we shall, for as soon as the mills and other apparatus get well to work, we shall be able to present substantial proof to refute the statements made by those who have...pronounced our country a "bilk," and our valuable mines a myth.

A third, and modest, form of local manifest destiny exaggeration was a series of reassuring squibs in which the editors reported their findings on location visits to the "diggings," or the optimism of interviewees. Examples are too numerous to cite fully; for instance, four in the May 30 issue and four in the June 6 issue alone. A random selection from a year and a half of publication should be enough:

> June 14, 1868: Buildings are rapidly going up in Atlantic City, showing the well-founded confidence its citizens have in the wealth of the surrounding quartz and placer claims....Ye poor miserable sceptics as to the wealth of our country, go over there and take a look for yourselves, and then, if you have any

knowledge of mining — you'll not expose yourself by denouncing the country's resources.

July 18, 1868: Yesterday we took a stroll down Willow Creek and had a good look at Mssrs. Tozer and Eddy's quartz mill, which is very nearly completed. We doubt if anywhere upon the Pacific Coast can be found (like this one) a quartz mill within a log building.

December 23, 1968 [published at Bryan City]: We had the pleasure of meeting Frank R. Judd, Esq., of Chicago, the other day. Mr. Judd paid our town a visit on business in regard to some mining interests in the Sweetwater country...he being an old Sweetwaterite, and, like all others who have been there, having perfect confidence in the mines, believing that it will be glorious.

And from *The South Pass News,* October 27, 1869:

ANOTHER STAMP MILL COMING — We are glad to learn that Mr. Pease...and also several others...has formed a company in Chicago for working these mines, and that one of those splendid engines and quartz mills has been ordered from the Eagle Works Manufacturing Company, P.W. Gates, President, Chicago.... There are a great number of mines discovered which "prospect" well, and nothing but capital and machinery is wanting to bring out their hidden riches. We believe that in less than six months half a score more of these quartz mills will be in process of erection in Sweetwater, and the proprietors of all coining money.

Actually it had become clear by the middle of the following summer, a little more than six months later, that the shallow deposits in the Sweetwater area would not pay for a large or permanent community, and that deep shaft mining would not yield a future. Warren and Hazard had been exaggerating all along, not to sell sensational sheets in which citizens could satisfy a lust for lawlessness, but to polish the image of democratic settlement in Sweetwater..

Research into Sweetwater newspapers inevitably leads back to the communities for which they were printed. Since only a few issues are extant, it is impossible to deduce anything about *The South Pass News,* but it is possible to say that in *The Sweetwater Mines* editorial policy and humor do not fit the conventional descriptions of frontier journalism. Is it equally possible to say that the communities were "different" from the ordinary mining community? There is ample evidence that South Pass City and Atlantic City little resembled the rip-roaring hell towns of popular history and grade B movies. In fact, by examining the real records and newspapers of other western mining communities, like Sweetwater's, not prey to commercialization in either century, future western scholars will probably find that neither Virginia City nor *The Territorial Enterprise* was "archetype" — only apogee. It is time to stop romanticizing our West; the truth was extraordinary enough. A new, calm, orderly look at the written evidence would be a first step. Court and commissioners' records lie untouched in archives while writers dig through earlier glamographs for "facts." The inside pages of old newspapers go unread by researchers eager to find lawlessness in flaring Page One headlines. The actual history of South Pass City, as of western mining settlement in general, has yet to be written.

1. See Bernard DeVoto, *Mark Twain's America,* Boston, 1932, p. 123. And Effie Mona Mack, *Mark Twain in Nevada,* New York, 1947, p. 183.

2. Mary Lou Pence and Lola Homsher, *The Ghost Towns of Wyoming,* New York, 1956, pp. 32-33.

3. Douglas McMurtrie, "Pioneer Printing in Wyoming," Cheyenne, 1933.

4. See Lola Homsher, *South Pass, 1868,* University of Nebraska Press, 1960, p. 218. Also, *The Mines,* May 27, 1868, advertisement: "1,000 laborers wanted to grade the railroad from Quaking Asp Mountain to the head of Echo Canyon...."

5. June 19, 1869. Atlantic City assayer Mr. Hahn was "severely wounded," the assailant claiming it accidental. The editors condemn the use of firearms while intoxicated, claiming there have been a number of similar incidents.

6. See Frank L. Mott, *American Journalism,* New York, 1941, p. 592.

7. Minutes of the County Commissioners, Carter County, Territory of Dakota, 1868-1870, University of Wyoming Library, Western History Division.

8. Constance Rourke, *American Humor,* "Facing West," New York, 1931.

9. "SM" refers to *The Sweetwater Mines,* "SPN" to *The South Pass News.* Each issue had five columns per page, each column 14½ inches vertically. There were twenty columns in four pages.

10. Henry Nash Smith's familiar analysis in *Virgin Land* documents and interprets this.

11. Though no census is available for 1868, it is reasonable to believe that South Pass City's population at no time exceeded 2,000, even including ancillary encampments along the streams and gulches.

12. Referring to the Wind River Valley region north of Sweetwater. Much harassed by Indians, poor transportation facilities and merciless winters, the few valley settlers were unable to develop a stable situation till the 1880's, long after Sweetwater had depopulated.

The Western Romantic Necessity in Literary Naturalism: Jack London

For the most part, the setting for American literary naturalism was the extended West — from the prairies of Ohio and Wisconsin, to the peaks of the Sierras. Jack London extended it to Alaska and the Pacific. In the works of Theodore Dreiser, Sherwood Anderson, Harold Frederic, E.W. Howe and Frank Norris, naturalism was used to dissect the social realities of small town and big city life all the way from the Ohio valley to the Sacramento Valley. The romantic necessity in this naturalism is related to the romance of lawlessness discussed in "Contradicting Romances in Western Writing."

What all these authors seem to be saying is that the corruptions and frustrations of their time are a legacy of frontier beginnings in which the development of the individual was glorified at the expense of the general good. It is only fitting that Herbert Croly published his influential *The Promise of American Life* in 1909, an important time for American literary naturalism. The work was to serve as ideological mainstay in the Progressive politics of Theodore Roosevelt, himself a glorifier of the West. The new novelists were showing character after character psychologically wracked by what Croly called "the special American political system." He defined the system as "indissolubly associated with the persistence of abundant and widely distributed economic prosperity." In Hamlin Garland's Wisconsin coulees,

in Theodore Dreiser's Chicago skyscrapers, and in Frank
Norris's California valleys, the "majority of good Americans"
that Croly talked about were not prosperous at all.[1] The more
they struggled against "natural" social and economic forces,
the more they corrupted themselves or were oppressed by
circumstances beyond their control. The original promise of
American life was that the use of the land would liberalize
society and free the man American to pursue his private
destiny. He must be ingenious, ruthless, practical, ambitious,
hard-headed. The original promise was embodied, for the West,
in the Romance of Lawlessness, which glorified such self-
centered enterprise. Contradictorily, that promise embodied
also the idea of collectivity in "democratic settlement." In
other words, the Western Hero was to exploit the free land for
himself then turn around and incorporate his individual
enterprise with that of his fellow men in peaceful mini-
republics. By 1909, American tradition had to face up to this
paradox, for, as literary naturalism saw it, the western hero
had become the mortgage holder and the corrupt entre-
preneur. The yeoman farmer, hero-intended of democratic
settlement, was under the exploiter's "paw," a victim of
countless "deals." From the sociological point of view,
Herbert Croly demanded a new set of myths and romances as
necessary modifications of original "individualism." Critic
George Soule summarized Croly's argument thus:

> The original American national purpose — a conscious attempt
> to liberate and enlarge the personality — had been perverted by
> self-seeking business and shallow politics, which made a hollow
> fetish of the doctrine that the Americans were a chosen people
> who were destined to achieve success by clinging to such
> traditional dogmas as natural rights and laissez faire.[2]

Croly concluded that more than anything else, in the first
decade of the Twentieth Century America needed a new
"social democratic ideal" which must embody both the
individualizing thrust that had made up so much of frontier
accomplishment, and the collectivizing thrust that had already
become important in shaping the American Twentieth Cen-

tury. The railroad tycoons excoriated by Frank Norris could only be controlled for the good of the farmer and small businessman by a force larger even than the corporation; and that would be the government.

But in western thinking, government has traditionally been the enemy, the long arm of Washington stifling free enterprise and ambition. Consequently, a central theme in western writing has always been the search for the fullest development of the free self — essentially a commercial variation on the existential search — within a working collective whole. Of all American naturalistic writers, Jack London most dramatically illustrates both the paradox itself and the search for a solution.

Jack London's work is most puzzling when viewed from the alleged opposition of naturalism and romanticism. From such a view Alfred Kazin remarks of London and Upton Sinclair, "the curious thing about these leading Socialist 'fictioneers' is that they were the most romantic novelists of their time."[3] But there is no fundamental mutual exclusiveness between modern romanticism and the modern view of a causative naturalist universe. In another paragraph Kazin unwittingly takes the curiousness out of the thing when he says that London's "heroes stormed the heights of their own minds, and shouted that they were storming the world."[4] Modern romanticism may be defined as the storming by private vision and power to comprehend and affect the universe; and London is, very simply, a romantic in his exultation of private visions which he takes to be visions of the modern world.

As every nineteenth-century man came to fear, and as every twentieth-century man has come to know, there are two worlds against which to storm: the supernatural and the natural. Perhaps in keeping with the modern temper these had better be called "forces." Faust fought the devil, but could not win against the supernatural force; Santiago, in Hemingway's *The Old Man and the Sea*, fought old age, the marlin's strength and will, and finally the marauder sharks, but could not win against these natural forces. Yet both these men are "heroes" of a private struggle against the forces that enclose them.

In the same way, Jack London's men fight, as heroes, against surrounding forces. But here we find a curious ambiguity: London depicts protagonists fighting to win in a causative naturalist universe; but he also depicts antagonists fighting to overcome the causative universe and to affirm beliefs not possible within the dialectics of that universe. For example, in *The Sea-Wolf* London presents two heroes: the titan Wolf Larsen and the "sissy" Humphrey Van Weyden. As narrator, Van Weyden introduces Wolf Larsen for his "strength," the kind "we are wont to associate with things primitive, with wild animals, and the creatures we imagine our tree-dwelling prototypes to have been — a strength savage, ferocious, alive in itself, the essence of life...the elemental stuff itself out of which the many forms of life have been molded." But this indomitable man, who literally snaps men's arms and legs with little effort, who emerges from a forecastle brawl — of which he is the intended victim — with no bruises, has a great weakness: he is worried. What is he worried about? He is worried about his own philosophy. When Van Weyden asks the atheist and Darwinian Larsen: "What do you believe, then?" he replies:

> "I believe that life is a mess...It is like yeast, a ferment, a thing
> that moves and may move for a minute, an hour, a year, or a
> hundred years, but that in the end will cease to move. The big
> eat the little that they may continue to move, the strong eat the
> weak that they may retain their strength. The lucky eat the
> most and move the longest, that is all."

His underlying uncertainty is indicated by the fact that he reads in the great classics — Shakespeare, Tennyson, Poe, De Quincey, Darwin, Tyndall, Bulfinch. Even more, there is evidence that Jack London himself is worried about Larsen's philosophy: though the first half of *The Sea-Wolf* is Larsen's story — the story of the strong man dominating the ship's little universe — it increasingly becomes the narrator's story as well. Humphrey Van Weyden is a man of civilization. He calls himself a "temperamental idealist" trying to put into speech "a something felt, a something like the strains of music heard in sleep, a something that convinced yet transcended utterance." In a few short weeks "Hump," as he is called, rises from bumbling cabin boy to effective first mate. He feels that his "hope and faith in human life still survived Wolf Larsen's destructive criticism," but he acknowledges that Larsen had been "a cause of change...had opened up for me the world of the real...from which I had always shrunk." Hump learns to defend himself against the threat of knifing, but also learns to answer Wolf's cruelty with strong-minded assertions of principle. Thus, two contrasting hero-types emerge: Larsen, accepting the naturalist universe, fighting only to be its master; and Hump, rejecting that universe, retaining his idealism and learning to fight against what he has rejected.

This ambiguity of heroes will be seen most strikingly in the character of Martin Eden, though earlier in his writing career, Jack London was able to avoid the ambiguity by the fortunate stroke of creating a non-human hero. In *The Call of the Wild*, Buck, the massive, powerful domestic animal, is gradually converted by the necessity to survive (The Law of Club and Fang) into the "dominant primordial beast." In Buck's universe, as in Wolf Larsen's, it is survive or die: "He must master or be mastered; while to show mercy was a weakness ....Kill or be killed, eat or be eaten, was the law; and this mandate, down out of the depths of Time, he obeyed." Gifted by nature with intelligence, physical strength and will, Buck conquers his enemy, Spitz, in a fight to the death, leads his pack of dogs in sled-harness, protects the man who saves him from the inhumanity of his former owners, avenges this man's death by killing his killers, then, compulsively, answers "the call of the wild" by becoming the dominant primordial beast among wild wolves. There is no ambiguity in Buck, the conquering hero in the naturalist universe. He does not read philosophers and poets; he does not suddenly develop a fatal cancer, as Wolf Larsen did. In a word, since he is only an animal, he can be only natural. *The Call of the Wild* is a perfect parable of a biologically and environmentally determined universe. There are no holes in the argument. Buck's highest achievement is to kill, till finally he achieves the killing of man, "the noblest game of all."

On the other hand, *The Call of the Wild* suggests the truth that a *wholly* naturalist human hero — operating in a wholly naturalist universe — is an impossibility. For then there could be no hero — no private vision — in a scheme that by definition precluded private variation. Such a scheme would remove from human beings their faculty for abstraction and for choice, that very faculty which raises them above the animal world, and we shall see in *Martin Eden* how London's own creeds of socialism and private knowledge inject romanticism into naturalism.

The hero struggling is the basic plot of literature. The private hero (or the mass as hero) either submits to supernatural or natural forces, or fights them.[5] If he fights, his personal conflict stands a fair chance to be worthy of "story." If he submits, there is no conflict; there is no story; there is no literature. In these terms, what is it that Martin Eden fights? What kind of hero is Martin Eden in the first place? Since *Martin Eden* is directly autobiographical, comment about Jack London's personal ideology is in order. In *The Liberation of American Literature*, V.F. Calverton says:

> he did not stop short with the petty bourgeois ideology of individualism but advanced to the collective philosophy of socialism. Had he stopped where most of his contemporaries did, and taken his stand upon an individualistic base, notwithstanding the personal energy he possessed, in all likelihood he would have been driven into the camp of the pessimists.... Instead, convinced as he became that socialism and not individualism was the philosophy that America, that the world, should adopt, he was able to escape in part that spiritual *cul de sac* in which most of his contemporaries were caught.[6]

It is true that as a Marxist literary critic Calverton has every reason to find less "pessimism" in London than general instability and early suicide might indicate. Calverton implies a consistency of view in London, a clarity of dedication, that the novelist lacked. London's life was a shambles of idealizations that personal neuroses often confused and defeated. Nevertheless, Calverton seems to have described the conflicting themes of London's autobiographical creation: the active theme, that rampant jungle law individualism was a "spiritual *cul de sac*," and the implied theme, that a "collective philosophy of socialism" (or something like it, something mutually committing and brotherhood-begetting) might provide fulfillment. Martin Eden's suicide becomes clearer when seen through the bi-focal lens of these themes. For Martin storms all the worlds before him, conquers each in turn, only to find that each victory carries within it the self-defeat of a blank future. As Martin himself says repeatedly, "Work performed," and as he asks himself in a dozen variations, "So what?"

In critical terms, Martin Eden is the protagonist storming the world as the hero of the Darwin-Spencer philosophy of individual survival; like Wolf Larsen, he is hero in the naturalist universe because he is its perfect embodiment. To the "petty bourgeois" assembled in the home of his sweetheart Ruth's father, Martin says:

> You still believe in equality, and yet you do the work of the corporations, and the corporations, from day to day, are busily engaged in burying equality. And you call me a Socialist because I want equality, because I affirm just what you live up to....As for myself, I am an individualist. I believe the race is to the swift, the battle to the strong. Such is the lesson I have learned from biology, or at least I think I have learned from biology. As I said, I am an individualist, and individualism is the hereditary and eternal foe of socialism.

What Martin really objects to is the hypocrisy, not the creed, of the bourgeois class. It is this hypocrisy, this shrinking in the face of total commitment to the jungle law, that he comes to hate in Ruth. Ironically, this reaction causes him to freeze her out of his life when finally he has succeeded in the bourgeois world by becoming a commercially successful author and thus "acceptable" to Ruth's family, and to her. In a word, Martin develops a strange idealism. He thinks of himself, after his tirade against the bourgeois, as "an intellectual moralist," and he finds "more offending to him than platitudinous pomposity...the morality of those about him, which was a curious hotch-potch of the economic, the metaphysical, the sentimental, and the imitative." The story of Martin Eden is, rather consistently, the story of the growth of this "intellectual morality," and the stillbirth of any "spiritual morality." This latter term is inadequate to what I mean, but I juxtapose it to the first term as a convenient way of expressing the "brotherhood" inherent in the socialism which London admired.

In the beginning, we see a type of "blond beast" who might go either way: might become the protagonist in a naturalist universe, like Wolf Larsen; or might become the antagonist against a naturalist universe, like Humphrey Van Weyden. London tells us that as Martin first walks into the bourgeois world his eyes show an "expression such as wild animals betray when they fear the trap." He is animal-like; at their first meeting, Ruth feels that "intense virility seemed to surge out from him and impinge upon her." Martin sees his primitive nature in terms of the women he has conquered: "frowsy, shuffling creatures from the pavements of Whitechapel, gin-bloated hags of the stews, and all...the scum and slime of the human pit." Then he sees Ruth as their antithesis, as civilized and ideally human: "Here was intellectual life, he thought, and here was beauty, warm and wonderful as he had never dreamed it could be....Here was something to live for, to win to, to fight for — ay, to die for..." And as his eyes scan the many books in the Morse household, in him rises "a wistfulness and a yearning as promptly as the yearning leaps into the eyes of a starving man at sight of food." Martin is hearing the heroic call to intellect, beauty, truth; and he answers this call of the unwild by determining, heroically enough, to live, fight, win, and if necessary, die to achieve them. The "high-pitched dominance of his nature" will not allow him to play second fiddle, so he will "win to the walk of life whereon she trod."

Intensely, Martin explores philosophy, science, mathematics. He wills himself forward despite lack of money and sometimes lack of food, till finally he makes "the great discovery," among "worldly socialists and working-class philosophers." We might expect this to be socialist-brotherhood commitment, and it does *sound* like the discovery of no less than Platonic idealism:

> What, in a way, most profoundly impressed Martin, was the correlation of knowledge — of all knowledge....He drew up lists of the most incongruous things and was unhappy until he succeeded in establishing kinship between them all — kinship between love, poetry, earthquake, fire, rattlesnakes....Thus, he unified the universe and held it up and looked at it...not as a terrified traveller in the thick of mysteries seeking an unknown goal....And the more he knew, the more passionately he admired the universe, and life, and his own life in the midst of it all.

In one reading, this is the universe of the *Theaetetus,* or perhaps the Transcendentalists; but there is a joker in the philosophical deck: Herbert Spencer. Martin discovers order in the Darwin-Spencer naturalist universe, where "the battle is to the strong" and individual striving and survival alone count. The "intellectual morality" which he develops confines him in this universe, so that the "spiritual morality" he might have embraced from his many exposures seems empty and worthless to him. His first conquest is the bourgeois, but he finds that he is disappointed. On the other hand, he is encouraged by his successes, for "the climb had been easier than he expected. He was superior to the climb." Now his "high-pitched dominance" impels him to conquer the field of writing. After his "great discovery" he proclaims to himself, "But cheer up, Martin, my boy. "You'll write yet. You know a little, a very little, and you're on the right road now to know more. Some day, if you're lucky, you may come pretty close to knowing all that may be known. Then you will write."

Write he does, despite the discouragement that when "he brought his great discovery to Ruth, sharing with her all his joy and wonder...she did not seem to be so enthusiastic over it." He reads every experience as confirmation of what

Spencer has taught him, so that every experience feeds his
compulsion to write Spencer's truths in a successful story. For
example, when he works with Joe Dawson at a resort laundry,
he calls the work "a great battle that continued under the
electric lights," but the battle deadens him, makes him feel
like a "work beast," and he leaves it.

He conquers the commercial (bourgeois) literary market,
to become a capitalist himself. Yet the same ironic process of
disillusion that taught him the bankruptcy of the bourgeois-
Ruth world of qualified individuality teaches him now the
bankruptcy of his writing success. The editors who would not
use his stuff earlier now compete individually and predatorily
for it. They degrade his friend Brissenden's long poem,
"Ephemera," by professional and commercial promotion.
Brissenden, who had no illusions about life — that is, placed
absolutely no value on living — had not wanted his poem
published. Watching its prostitution, after Brissenden's suicide,
Martin begins to accept that pessimism:

> "Pretty good thing you died, Briss, old man," Martin
> murmured, letting the magazine slip between his knees to the
> floor.
>
> The cheapness and vulgarity of it was nauseating, and Martin
> noted apathetically that he was not nauseated very much. He
> wished he could get angry, but did not have energy enough to
> try. He was too numb....After all, what did it matter? It was on
> a par with all the rest that Brissenden had condemned in
> bourgeois society.
>
> "Poor Briss," Martin commented; "he would never have
> forgiven me [for promoting its publication]."

Martin is apathetic because he has succeeded again in his
rampant individuality only to find the success again worthless.
So he begins a half-hearted re-exploration of values. He stops
at a bricklayer's picnic where he meets Lizzie, a factory girl
who had wanted him early in the story and who, it turns out,
still loves him. He thrills to the fight that Lizzie's escort starts
with him, and he wins Lizzie away with the help of his
admiring working class friends. Lizzie's loyalty makes her

"great and noble" in his eyes. He tells her sincerely, "You are a ray of light to me in a very dark world." From her first glance "he knew she was his, that all he had to do was say 'Come,' and she would go with him all over the world wherever he led." But this unqualified love — "You could do anything with me. You could throw me in the dirt an' walk on me" — now looks to Martin like more of the same "battle to the strong" conquest, and for that reason he decides not to accept it.

At this point Martin in effect gives up his naturalist philosophy. Attempting to compensate for its excesses, he becomes the altruist: sends Lizzie to night school; buys his landlady Maria the rooming house and chicken farm she wants; gives his sister Gertrude all the money he owes her and more; and even agrees to pay for remodeling her husband's store (though he thoroughly hates Bernard) on the promise that Gertrude will never have to overwork again. Finally, he buys his old friend Joe Dawson a laundry. But we see Martin's altruism, and his feeling of emptiness, most forcefully when Kreis, one of the group with whom Martin had shared one night of intense intellectual excitement, comes to ask for a thousand dollars. Making out the check, Martin reminds Kreis of that night and Kreis offers to provide more of them. Martin replies, "Too late. That night was the one night for me. I was in paradise....I shall never live at such a pitch again. I'm done with Philosophy. I want never to hear another word of it."

The hero has fallen, having conquered — nothing. Finally he tries, but without enthusiasm, to recapture his violent zest for individual fulfillment by returning to the South Seas. En route, he drowns himself. The commitment to others that he half-heartedly began to play out, toward the end, did not open up to him the faith that mutuality was worth living for. He did not quite learn or perhaps could not quite bear to believe, that he might turn about and fight the false universe he had accepted. On the flyleaf of a copy of *Martin Eden* that London is supposed to have sent Upton Sinclair, the author wrote, "One of my motifs in *Martin Eden* was an attack on individualism."[7]

Thus we see that London was unable to formulate a new American promise, unable to gain faith in what Herbert Croly had called the new "social democratic ideal." Croly's faith was essentially "liberal," though he disavowed the term in later life. In the tradition of John Locke, Thomas Jefferson and John Stuart Mill, he believed that men could arrange their collective destinies liveably and peaceably on earth. Like many European and some American literary naturalists, London died believing that the law of club and fang would necessarily pervert all social promise to individual ends. To this brand of naturalist, the only worthwhile struggle is the individual's, against an implacable set of natural forces; and this is still the implied but powerful land-bound ideological limitation of thinking centered in the American West.

1. Herbert Croly, *The Promise of American Life*, New York, 1964, p. 11.

2. George Soule, *Encyclopedia of the Social Sciences*, New York, 1931, Vol. IV, p. 603.

3. Alfred Kazin, *On Native Grounds*, New York, 1942, p. 110.

4. *Ibid.*, p. 115.

5. The mass hero, as portrayed in Zola's *Germinal* and in the horrifying massacre chapters of London's *The Iron Heel*, might well be analyzed on the same basis as the private hero.

6. V. F. Calverton, *The Liberation of American Literature*, New York, 1932, p. 419.

7. Cited in Irving Stone, *Sailor on Horseback*, Cambridge, 1938, p. 259.

The Unwritten West

Before the results of western achievement had settled sufficiently to make out the esthetics behind the smoke and dust, entertainment began simplifying "The Great West" into "The Wild West." In this century the parody was perfected by radio, paperbacks, pulps, movies, and television. From the beginning the complex region west of the Mississippi-Missouri has been deprived of the dignity of reality. The same process, reducing history to cheap myth, has made serious teaching about the West nearly impossible at all levels, including the university. The text writers glamorize — even fantasize — out of all bounds writing about the trails, cattle drives, mining towns, and Indians. Like their own children they are addicted to the comic-book Romance of Lawlessness, America's most popular and absurd self-glorification.

In this Romance, violations of law and disrespect for community are supposed to have been abnormally justified by the western environment. It is one thing to maintain that lawlessness was abnormally present during settlement but quite another to assume that it morally befit that settlement. Bernard DeVoto is a classic example of this systematic distortion; in entertainment, Mark Twain is another. Since the chief end of entertainment is to create fantasy out of reality, Twain cannot be blamed for his excesses, but scholars and artists can. In literature especially, the Romance has reduced art to entertainment.

Public, scholarly, and artistic traditions to the contrary

61

however, art is no less possible for the West than for the other regions. Important emotions can be evoked; the great questions can be asked in the West. As a matter of fact a handful of writers have begun to ask them, providing some powerful answers. There is no literary movement yet, but at least there is motion. Luckily the critics have worried a great deal more about the misuse of the West in American art than have the writers. For instance, the critics wonder why Whitman's vision has seen so little fulfillment: "Yes, I think the chyle of not only poetry and painting, but oratory, and even the metaphysics and music fit for the New World, before being finally assimilated, need first and feeding visits here."

Critics suggest at least three answers. First, the overwhelming geography of the area may reduce the mind from metaphysical to merely physical capability. Thomas Hornsby Ferril, Colorado poet and critic, feels: "Rocky Mountain literature is devitalized by a low-grade mysticism dictated by landscape....The imagination, transported to enormous mountains, deserts and canyons, endeavors to answer landscape directly and tends to disregard, or curiously modify, what might otherwise be normal considerations of human experience." He cites Oscar Wilde's tempting analogy between the West and Switzerland: "The mountains...are so gigantic that they are not favorable to art or poetry."

Another answer is the vernacular roots that have nourished nearly all middlewestern and western art. American Studies specialist Leo Marx feels that "the vernacular style is a distinctive achievement of American culture. But this is not to say that it has served to convey anything like an adequate view of experience, or that it has yet given America a great literature." Marx feels that its emphasis on primitivist sources has led to "the chief defect of the vernacular mode — its unremitting anti-intellectualism," a bias of our own time.

The third explanation takes up where Fredrick Jackson Turner left off, emphasizing not the settlement of the West but the lateness of that settlement at a time of growing national and international tensions. There is real truth in the familiar observation that the weeklies hoarded western materials to feed an eastern population hungry to escape the industrial, political, and social disturbances that quickly intensified after the Civil War. Mark Twain wrote *Roughing It* for his eastern audience; *Harper's, DeBow's Review, Century Magazine,* and nearly every other popular printed outlet commissioned artists, illustrators and writers by the score (sometimes in teams) to furnish the East with western exotica — Frederic Remington and Twain are only two of the most famous. Locals like Mary Foote of Denver found thirsty markets for their word and picture barbiturates of frontier life. Geologists, historians, and laymen made minor fortunes with their "journals" of "real life" in the settler, cattle, mining, and Indian territories — Francis Parkman is only the most famous of these. Guide books full of statistics, testimony, and practical traveling advice were printed and reprinted, revised and advertised. So what was the image stamped on American thought? The titles and preface of C.W. Dana's *The Great West, or the Garden of the World; Its History, Its Wealth, Its Natural Advantages, And Its Future, also comprising A Complete Guide to Emigrants, with A Full Description of the Different Routes Westward* (1858), are representative:

> The Land of Promise, and the Canaan of our time, is the region which, commencing on the slope of the Alleghenies, broadens grandly over the vast prairies and mighty rivers, over queenly lakes and lofty mountains, until the ebb and flow of the Pacific tide kisses the golden shores of the El Dorado.
>
> With a soil more fertile than human agriculture has yet tilled; with a climate balmy and healthful, such as no other land in other zones can claim; with facilities for internal communication which outrival the world in extent and grandeur, — it does indeed present to the nations a land where the wildest dreamer on the future of our race may one day see actualized a destiny far outreaching in splendour his most gorgeous visions.

Clearly, the myths of the West developed mainly in the East; just as clearly, their romantic, escapist satisfactions are magnetic to our own time. For this reason the usual reaction to a proposed "serious" story, script, or scholarly paper with a western theme is "Oh yes, that sounds interesting — the only trouble is, it's been done *so much*!"

In truth, it's been done *very little*! The great questions have almost never been asked in the West: right and wrong, good and evil, vision and blindness, commitment and detachment, love and lust. Though more guns have blazed in the fairy-tale West than ever blazed in a war, hardly a single conflict has been portrayed. Though every kind of human experience has actually been felt and played out there, few have been recreated by art. Thomas Hornsby Ferril sees the paradox when he says, "It is not drawing too long a bow to regard the galloping heroes of popular fiction as vestigial tribal gods. They have emerged through about the same process which once produced centaurs and titans, but their development has been arrested at a rudimentary plane." As images, the western centaurs and titans are little more than ludicrous to the eye, their flat dialects an offense to the ear. Surrounded by movies, television, and paperbacks, we can hardly escape the parody which, because unconscious and devoted to the making of money, lacks the humor of decent parody or the pathos of burlesque. We are out of patience with dark-dressed badmen, sandy-haired good marshals, hoe-carrying, feet-apart settlers, hyperthyroid gunslingers, and the curious collection of noble savage and slit-eyed voluptuary known as "The American Indian." Yet there were no doubt gunslingers who worried about the moral implications of their work, acute and hyperthyroid farmers, and "savages" whose nobility fought great battles of right and wrong with their customs and angers.

As a matter of fact, such writers as Walter Van Tilburg Clark, H.L. Davis, Willa Cather, and A.B. Guthrie, Jr.; such poets as Carl Sandburg, Thomas Hornsby Ferril, and Alan Swallow; and such artists as Maynard Dixon, C.S. Price, Tom Lea, and the members of the Taos School have already begun the important work of using western images for metaphors of human experience: scattered but significant attempts to transcend and restate Daniel Boone, Kit Carson, or Burralo Bill. Within the compound sentence structure that dominates

the American paragraph, the descriptions of arroyos, sheepmen, tumultuous hooves, and pine-studded evenings are
sometimes being properly used — as backgrounds for testing
human values in the light and dark of a mighty environment. A
reading of H.L. Davis' short story, "Open Winter," is a
testimony. Its main characters, Old Apling and Young Beech,
stand in the classical pattern of age to youth, method to
impatience — but with this difference: age passes on values,
not gun practice, to youth. As the story opens the two men
have just driven a small herd of half-starved horses back to
their owner after pasturing them on Old Apling's spread for a
contracted sum, only to find that their owner, Gervais, has left
both the area and the contract debt. Out of spite, young Beech
wants to abandon the horses to probable starvation, but Old
Apling insists they have a duty to the horses, and more, to
their sense of right:

> Ream Gervais don't count in this....What does he care about
> those horses? What counts is you, and I don't have to think up
> any better argument, because I've already got one. You may not
> realise it, but you and me are responsible for these horses till
> they're delivered to their owner....It's against the law to let
> horses starve to death, did you know that? If you pull out of
> here I'll put out right along with you, and I'll have every man in
> that town after you before the week's out.

From such an apparently typical "western" threat we
might well expect the old posse-after-outlaw game to follow;
but there is no posse, and though young Beech does finally
pull out, he returns after protecting both Old Apling and the
horses from unfriendly sheepmen. Even had there been a posse
(as there so effectively is in a somewhat parallel tale, Walter
Van Tilburg Clark's *The Ox-Bow Incident*) notice the issues at
stake: recklessness and obligation. Young Beech learns a
number of lessons in the trip down to the Columbia Valley
(where they believe Gervais has moved). He learns to find
water in a dry arroyo, but he also learns to find responsibility.

The *Ox-Bow Incident* is the classic of the recent attempt
to restate the West. In part, the work fails this grand,

consciously undertaken task, but Mr. Clark was playing for high stakes, as a few years later A.B. Guthrie, Jr., was to play for the same high stakes in *The Big Sky.* It is not necessary to recount at length the obviously classical structure of The *Ox-Bow Incident* — how Wrong inexorably, in the name of Law, inflicts injustice on the innocent, whose Right is corrupted by Circumstance to appear as Lawlessness. Every important western stereotype except the Indian is given a part on this dark Nevada stage: the power maniac, the mannish-woman leader, the single-minded humorless cattleman, the sympathetic barkeep, the ignorant cowboy, the weak dude, the loose girl, the earnest young settler, the canny Mexican and so on. But for once in a western tale the characters interact toward an ironic, not a mechanically romantic outcome: though the reader, out of habit, keeps expecting the usual forces — the "hero," the sheriff, the dead-man-not-dead — to free the tight play from its tragic final act, his compassion is not appeased. It is to Clark's everlasting credit that though nearly all the members of the posse, every reader, and fifteen years of movie audiences have not wanted Wrong to call the final shot, it nevertheless does. The innocents die at the unjust hand of Justice, and the moment of their strangulation on the bough of the ox-bow tree in the fierce Sierra has proved historic for the future of western literature. Here the reader is stimulated and frightened in a new way by new people: westerners working at great moral questions.

In *The Ox-Bow Incident* Clark takes on but does not bring to the mat the other important problems that future western art must wrestle with. His characters, discoursing in the vernacular on subjects that worried Socrates, are meant as dots in a tiny drama that find its logos in the grandest dramas — the religious dramas. If they ask their questions rhetorically, debating not in high music but meandering dialogue, so that finally we feel that they take too long to get to their horses, we are bound also to feel that these are important questions with at best uneasy answers. We cannot help leaving *The Ox-Bow Incident* (especially the less talky, more dramatic movie version) with an uplifted feeling of participation in matters bordering on the eternal. The unresolved clash between vernacular and universal which is probably responsible for the artistic shortcomings of the work is less important for the audience than its overall success and is quite challenging for the artist in its esthetic implications. As Leo Marx suggests, the vernacular writer takes great risks, the western vernacular writer especially, for he must not only do the important but undo the silly.

These examples labor the obvious: cliches bury but do not murder truth. The absurdities of earlier western art and the limitations of current attempts should not discourage the American artist but should inspire him as the explorer is inspired, to line out an uncharted map. There are great blanks in the American literary map besides the cowboy and settler West; the most important is the Indian. To be sure, we still patronize him, finding our sermon in two distinct texts: the studies of the anthropologists and the entertainment media. We still rationalize that though what we did was awful, he *was* socially, intellectually, and materially unequipped to survive in modern civilization!

We are painfully aware, though, on some deep level, of the tragedy's prominent place among the unholy testaments. How is it then, that we must perpetually endure the teepee-wampum-ugh portrayal of dark, waxy objects to be shot down by "heroic" whites? How is it we cannot find in our entire literature an Indian who is a man before he is an aborigine? Only occasionally, as in the movie *The Broken Arrow,* and the novels *Little Big Man* and *Stay Away Joe* does a writer sneak some breath into a redman's lungs, and the result is a revelation. The answer is, of course, that the purveyors continue to ignore the tragedy in favor of the travesty because their ignoring is well rewarded at the box office.

Has a single major writer, playwright, or scenarist yet attempted to deal with this tragedy in its valuative, emotional, high terms? The author of a fairly recent addition to the Custer myth tells us:

There is, I believe, no incident in American history that has
been made the subject of more research, investigation and
speculation than the battle of the Little Big Horn, which was
the culmination of Custer's career, and in which he and his men
reached the end of the trail. Hundreds — indeed thousands — of
books, pamphlets, magazine articles and newspaper stories have
been written about it; some of them good, more of them bad,
and still more, indifferent. And the end is not yet.

The battle itself has starred; drama has been counted in
numbers of soldiers lost. In all the smoke-and-blood fuss no
one seems to have taken account of the enormous moral
necessity betrayed at this particular climax. To the objection
that the American artist and audience have had enough of
noble savages, the reply is resounding agreement. The noble
savage is basically a patronization anyway. But the American
artist and audience have had almost nothing yet of the
American Indian human, trapped and flailing, magnificent and
cowardly, ignorant and wise, limited and passionate.

As a matter of fact, one of the most moving bits of recent
writing about the Indian is set in a Great Plains cabin, not on a
battlefield, and has for its main characters a white man
without his boots on and an Indian girl who says absolutely
nothing at all — not even "ugh." Precisely because he has gone
in search of tormented souls, Ernest Haycox has given us an
important clue to the possibilities of western art in his brief
story, "A Question of Blood." Frank Isabel, a recent settler,
has bought an Indian wife for a horse and a quart of whiskey.
As cattlemen begin filling up the area earlier "held" by
trappers, Haycox depicts western human geography in its
typical genesis; but Isabel is no cardboard settler, the Crow girl
no wax model, and their life is a mixture of warmth and
silence. Though Isabel feels he can never get at the thoughts of
the dark girl crouching in a dark corner of the room — he
barely speaks her language and she, English not at all — he is
actually sensitive and compassionate. Otherwise he would not
have taken her three hundred miles to Cheyenne for a
"regular" marriage just before their child was born; and he

would not have told her, on their visit to the new town that
has sprung up in the plains nearby, "Those men are fools, I am
not ashamed of you." But of course he is, for the odor of the
blanket is upon him, and his kind do not hide their sniffing.
Sensing Isabel's fear of ridicule and his growing shame, the
Crow girl begins eating on a floor blanket again, setting the
child's place beside her. Their worlds wander from each other
as Isabel frets about the future life of the child in an intolerant
white world. One night a friend drops in, and on leaving,
remarks, "Your youngster's growin' up, Frank." The judgment
implied in the casual remark decides Isabel: he brings another
chair to the table and sets the child in it. He is "a long man
throwing a thin shadow across the room," while his Indian
wife draws "farther and farther back into the corner, like a
shadow vanishing. And then, with his face turned suddenly
away, he heard her stifled and terrible crying tremble the
room's silence."

Though the last lines have the rhythm of aching inevita-
bility, the story is merely a sketch, its impact limited. Frank
Isabel is more than a cardboard cutout but not quite a
sympathetic breathing human; the Crow girl is more than a
figurine, yet she never quite engages our emotions because we
are never exposed to her thoughts, and not even to her
emotions, till the final sentence. So "A Question of Blood" is
more important for what it could have been than for what it
is. Whether accidentally or by design, the author has employed
the worn-out settler and Indian-maiden images in a dramatic
(domestic) treatment that is almost metaphorical of the Indian
ordeal.

Texts must not only be taken from the West, they must be
brought to it. Not merely the realistic and naturalistic texts of
the last two generations but the lyric, picaresque, morality,
history, and sonnet texts are needed also. It might be argued
that these would reinforce flatulent myth-making, but
myth-making for entertainment is distinct from myth-making
for art. Great poets must have great audiences, as Whitman
said, and can have them: there is nothing exclusive in the

world's appreciation of *Hamlet.* On the other hand, mass culture need not preclude art for the inner tastes. We are fed up with both the worn romanticism of western entertainment myths and the rutted naturalism of modern literature. In the deadly exploitation of both approaches, the writer is imposing his limitations on the American public, not the public on him. The liberated perception will not find ludicrous the suggestion that Oedipus might be very much at home on a major Rockies ranch if conducted there by an artist of sufficient genius. For west of explored America, there have been empires of enormous scope with fates, foibles, and fortunes of national breadth and intensity not fundamentally less human or divine than those in Asia, Europe, or the eastern half of the United States.

It is time to begin again with the true materials of American culture, not the tried ones. Every age must accept the passing of its esthetic frontiers, not merely their forms but their materials. Seventy-five years ago the American writer became obsessed with disruption, chaos, disbelief, and for perfectly sound reasons, but in 1974 we find ourselves unannihilated. There are faint lines of progress; the great issues have not destroyed us. We have reason to curb pessimism but are too used to it. We have lost our creative strength to it. The American writer must not separate himself from "reality," but he must recognize the dearth of important matter in his literature today. Freud, Marx, Jake Barnes, and Blanche DuBois have been fed into the young imagination till it is glutted, yet ironically suffers from malnutrition. It is time to take up the great questions all over again. This time, Whitman may have been right: American writing may make its future "feeding visits" to the American West.

Style in the Literary Desert: Mary Austin

Mary Austin grew up in Illinois, but tells us in her autobiography, *Earth Horizon,* that her real life began in California. From 1893 till her death in 1934, Miss Austin identified herself with a broad geography and a broad range of literary and political causes. She roamed and lived in the mountains and deserts of California, Nevada, Arizona and New Mexico; joined artists' colonies in Carmel and Taos; plunked for women's rights, and for freer expression in literature. She published over thirty volumes of novels, short stories, studies and plays; learned at close range the beauties and complexities of Indian lore, chant and song, and embodied these in a classic treatment, *The American Rhythm,* and in a full-length play, *The Arrow-Maker.*

Today, none of her works are in print, partly because they fit no established category of western writing, and partly because many of them were second rate. However, in one volume of short stories, *Lost Borders,* Miss Austin discovered workable myth in the timelessness of life as she felt and saw it in the southwestern desert. The literary consequences of this discovery are significant because in *Lost Borders* she was able to bring western writing into a great tradition with a quality that has seldom been duplicated. Henry Nash Smith called her a literary mystic who believed that the American landscape had "the power...to influence form."[1] She understood that the West had the power to influence, first, the form of its human life, and second, the shape of its human myths. So have a host of entertainers and commentators from Timothy Flint to today's television script writers. The crucial difference was her insistence on literary *form*, and with the publication of *Lost Borders* in 1909, Mary Austin brought style and sensibility to the literary raw materials of the West.

As a mystic, Mary Austin both required myth and newly revealed it. In her autobiography, *Earth Horizon,* she explained that her literary revelation was based on the certainty that "the story pattern is older than man...the story as communication between creature and creature is an older function of story art than the schools had thought."[2] She recalled hunting dogs "following the talk" in the gunroom:

> What Mary could not help but notice was that the dogs listened most attentively, participating, to the fullest extent, in stories of experienced events, such as a lost scent or elusive game retrieved under difficulties. Words, even the words that made up their common vocabulary...interested them not much, but a whole pattern of signs and sounds arranged around an event made that event live again for them; automatically accompanied by its original automatic reaction.[3]

Her myth interest, then, was to find the universal in inanimate and animate "landscape," and her stylistic interest was to "arrange" sights and sounds "around an event" so that it could live again. She understood that to become art, myth required style, and in *Lost Borders* she provided it.

The components of this style seem at first curiously at odds with the overwhelming physique of the western landscape. We do not normally think of the West by inference, indefiniteness, or metaphor; in the mode of ambiguity. However, Mary Austin did, and her style in *Lost Borders* is close in tone and technique to that of Hawthorne, Henry James and Hemingway. While these authors for the most part arranged sights and sounds around the urban "event," Mary Austin's landscape is rural in the extreme sense; and so is her style. In all these authors, style developed partly out of a keen myth-sense: the "hidden heart" of Hawthorne, the "felt life" of James, the "honor" of Hemingway. Since hers is a myth of timelessness, the "sights and sounds" of her California desert and its people suggest suspension, incompleteness, and intuitive, not rational, order. As in Henry James and Hemingway, a great deal is never told, but is hinted at. Her style, like James's, depends on a distillation of experience through a single articulate point of view. The thirteen short stories are held together first, by the author's constant presence as involved narrator; second, by her continual explicit attempts to gather the "sticks and straws" of events; and third, as in *In Our Time*, by the connecting commentaries which impose a loose unity.

Myth-gathering is not easy, though, and throughout the stories the narrator travels in conscious search. The sense of eternal, primal myth is heightened by her inability ever "to come upon a story all at once." For example, in "Agua Duice" the stage driver intrigues her by beginning a story about a young white and an Indian girl. When he stops talking she notes, "There was a good hour yet until we came to Coyote Pass; and I meant to have it all out of him by then." At the beginning of "The Woman at the Eighteen-Mile" she tells us: "I had long wished to write a story of Death Valley that should be its final word....And from the moment of hearing of the finding of Lang's body at Dead Man's Spring I knew I had struck upon the trail of that story." But the teamster who began the story was slow, big, blunt, and

> the same accident that had flattened the outlines of his nose and chin must have happened to his mind, for he was never able to deliver more than the middle of an idea, without any definiteness as to where it began or ended, and what it stood next to. He called the dead man Long [instead of Lang], and failed to remember who was supposed to have killed him, and what about.

The story-gatherer is by necessity a professional busybody. Working to gather up the loose ends of the teamster's story, she "heard of [it] again between Red Rock and Coyote Holes, about moon-set, when the stage labored up a long gorge...." Since the passengers only know part of it, "I went about asking for it." A barkeep in Tio Juan provides a patch of evidence concerning "Whitmark's dealing with the Shoshone who was supposed to have stolen the body after it was dug up." Again as in Henry James, the reader and the narrator have gone along together in their uncertainties; Mrs. Austin creates suspense by not disclosing who Whitmark or Lang were; or what the violence was about. The narrator soon hears of a Mexican who was supposed to have been the last to see the man alive, "but death got him before I did." Later, at a San Francisco dinner, another man remarks to her, "Queer thing happened up in that country to a friend of mine, Whitmark—;" but, she adds, "The toastmaster cut *him* off."

At this point Mrs. Austin gathers matters together for us, investing them with the quality if not the continuity of story:

> It had warmth and amplitude, like a thing palpable to be stroked. There was a mine in it, a murder and a mystery, great sacrifice, Shoshones, dark and incredibly discreet...there were lonely water holes, deserted camps where coyotes hunted in the streets, fatigues and dreams and voices of the night. And at the last it appeared there was a woman in it.

In a number of significant ways the introduction of the Woman of the Eighteen Mile has been unusual in western American fiction, because her story has not been lined out in typically geographical and melodramatic western terms: it has not been overexposed. The "mine," "murder," "mystery," "sacrifice," "Shoshones," "water-holes," "deserted camps," "fatigues," "dreams," and "voices" have taken on a metaphoric quality because they have not been described, but sensed. The woman is herself presented as a being sensed, rather than understood: "She had been, at the time [her husband] came into the country seventeen years before, that which the world knows so little what to do with that it mostly throws away — a good woman with great power and possibilities of passion."

She is also presented graphically: "She has the desert mark upon her — lean figure, wasted bosom, the sharp, upright furrow between the eyes, the burned, tawny skin, with the pallid streak of the dropped eyelids...." The description seems at first so familiar to western story that it borders on cliche. But the first instance of her presence — on the night the narrator "gets the rest of it" — cancels the possibility of cliche, for it has incompleteness, indefiniteness, mystery, and a little miracle:

> Never mind what went before to draw her to the point of talking; it could have come about as simply as my saying, "I mean to print this story as I find it," and she would have had to talk to save it....Consider how still it was....Not a leaf to rustle, not a bough to break. No grass to whisper in the wind, only stiff, scant shrubs and the sandy hills like shoals at the bottom of a lake of light. I could see the Woman's profile thin and fine against the moon, and when she put up her head to drag down the thick, careless coil of her hair, I guessed we were close upon the heart of her story.

Style has become explicit here — the landscape has influenced the form, and the Woman's dramatic moment is suspended, figuratively, "at the bottom of a lake of light," and it is aesthetically logical that the words Mary Austin chose, themselves have unity of sound. As in Hawthorne, James and Hemingway, the removal from literal "telling" has freed the imagination to select sound impressions that beautify sense impressions; an unusual sensibility in Western American writing. The description of the right landscape is filled with alliteration and assonance, as is the brief picture of the Woman at her point of revelation. The sequence of related sounds unites the two descriptions, as the situation has fused the landscape and its human presences.

This interworking of sensibility and style to create out of the familiar Western landscape a figurative dimension, can be seen in every one of the *Lost Borders* stories. In "The Ploughed Lands" Cavin sets out in spring, "all the air soft as shed petals." Losing his way, he fights thirst and starvation, and "There came a time...when the one consuming desire of the man was to get shut of the whole affair, the swimming earth that swung and tilted about the pivot of his feet...." In "The Last Antelope," the shepherd returns with his sheep to the Ceriso area in late summer, "by the time the poppy fires were quite burned out and the quail trooped at noon about the tepid pools." Describing an old antelope in the same story, Mrs. Austin creates a sound pattern that evokes and therefore does not need to state, loneliness: "...the antelope delayed his coming until the salt pool shrunk to its innermost ring of reeds, and the sun-cured grasses crisped along the slope." Again, in the beginning of "The Walking Woman" Mrs. Austin makes images and sounds reinforce each other to create an unforgettable sense of movement in desert heat:

> We had come all one day between blunt, whitish bluffs rising from mirage water, with a thin, pale wake of dust billowing from the wheels, all the dead wall of the foothills sliding and shimmering with heat, to learn that the Walking Woman had passed us somewhere in the dizzying dimness, going down to the Tulares on her own feet.

The consonants "w," "b," "d," and "l" combine with variations of "a" and "u" sounds to unify the images in our sight and our imagination.

Of the thirteen stories in *Lost Borders*, "The Walking Woman" most thoroughly illustrates the high level of Mrs. Austin's achievement. It begins with a characteristically sharp, but *in*definite statement: "The first time of my hearing of her was at Temblor." Further name and place details are piled up as the narrator hunts down the story:

> We heard of her again in Carrisal...where she had passed the week before shearing....

> She was at Maverick the time of the Big Snow, and at Tres Pinos when they brought home the body of Morena....

> She had eaten and slept at the herder's camps, and laid by for days at one-man stations whose masters had no other touch of human kind than the passing of chance prospectors, or the halting of the tri-weekly stage.

These narrative "sticks and straws" communicate the timeless *quality* of the landscape precisely because they are not described; they must be imagined. In turn, the imagination allows a world in which an uncommon wanderer like The Walking Woman is possible: "She came and went, oftenest in a kind of muse of travel which the untrammeled space begets, or at rare intervals flooding wonderously with talk, never of herself, but of things she had known and seen." The Walking Woman is no stereotype of western American woman, yet she is believably human. Mrs. Austin's next description gives us insight into this woman in a wholly realistic way: "She had been set on her way by teamsters who lifted her out of white, hot desertness and put her down at the crossing of unnamed ways, days distant from anywhere. And through all this she had passed unarmed and unoffended. I had the best testimony of this, the men themselves." Mrs. Austin then complicates the picture with "contradictions of reports of her." Some said she was comely, others that she was plain to the point of deformity; some said that she had a twist to her face, a hitch to her shoulder, and a definite limp. Yet, the author adds, "By the distance she covered she should have been straight and young." Some thought she was insane, and on "the evidence of her way of life she was cracked." Yet others pointed out that "in her talk there was both wisdom and information, and the word she brought about trails and waterholes was as reliable as an Indian's." Apparently, so the legend goes, to cure either a physical or mental illness brought on by long years of caring for an invalid — no one knows who this might have been — she took to walking with only a black bag and blanket hung from a stick. To this point the entire portrait is skillfully ambiguous: she is sane and insane, deformed and comely, and the invalid might well have been her own mind. Thus her march along the borders of civilization seems a symbolic pilgrimage to find self. This kind of theme is not usually applied to the landscape of the American desert.

The author contributes her own testimony, not to clarify the ambiguity, but to thicken it. "At the time I knew her, though she wore short hair and a man's boots, and had a fine down all over her face from exposure to the weather, she was perfectly sweet and sane." Less than halfway through the story, the author and the Walking Woman finally talk. "It was at Warm Spring in the Little Antelope I came upon her in the heart of a clear forenoon....The best of our talk that day began in some dropped word of hers from which I inferred that she had a child." The meeting takes place accidentally mid-desert, and the conversation begins accidentally; as in Hemingway, talk creates the metaphorical world.

At first the author is surprised about the child, but then wonders at her own reaction, "for it is the most natural of all experiences to have children." Like the reader, the author senses the dual human situation the Walking Woman symbolizes: individuality and society. When the author expresses her reaction, the Walking Woman explains her private philosophy: "...there were three things which if you had known you could cut out all the rest, and they were good any way you got them, but best if, as in her case, they were related to and grew each one out of the others." The first is the simple working together of man and woman as natural equals. She tells how she and a sheepherder, Filon, kept together a flock for a whole day during a sandstorm:

> And I was not tired....For you see, I worked with a man, without excusing, without any burden on me of looking or seeming. No fiddling or fumbling as women work, and hoping it will turn out for the best. It was not for Filon to ask, Can you, or Will you. He said, Do, and I did. And my work was good. We held the flock. And that is one of the things that make you able to do without the others.

The Walking Woman then tells what "the others" are, by picturing the moments after the storm passed and the flock began to feed again:

> We were very comfortable, and not so tired as we expected to be. Filon leaned up on his elbow. I had not noticed till then how broad he was in the shoulders, and how strong in the arms. And we had saved the flock together. We felt that....The wind was stopped, and all the earth smelled of dust, and Filon understood very well what I had done with him I could not have done so well with another. And the look — the look in his eyes —

At this point Mrs. Austin achieves a psychologically realistic if unexpected stroke: the Walking Woman touches her, as if the second of the three natural miracles must be communicated, as it was brought about, by the touch of bodies. The indirection and incompleteness with which the second of the three things is presented makes it more believably whole than physical description could possibly have done. Withdrawing her hand, the Walking Woman goes on: "To work together, to love together; there you have two of the things; the other you know."

The author knows: "The mouth at the breast."

"The lips and the hands," adds the Walking Woman. "The little, pushing hands and the small cry." Clearly these details have by now taken on metaphorically value: not simply the actions of adults and an infant, but suggestions of the spirit. The landscape description that follows delicately reinforces the mythic sense toward which the Walking Woman's personal revelation has been developing: "There ensued a pause of fullest understanding, while the land before us swam in the noon, and a dove in the oaks behind the spring began to call. A little red fox came out of the hills and lapped delicately at the pool." After adding that she had stayed happily with Filon till the child was born, and that the child had died shortly after, the Walking Woman leaves the author "as outliers do, without hope expressed of another meeting and no word of good-bye." The sense of timelessness is suggested by the character's seeming innocence of the need for continuity:

> She was the Walking Woman. That was it. She had walked off all sense of society-made values, and, knowing the best when the best came to her, was able to take it. Work — as I believed; love — as the Walking Woman had proved it; a child — as you subscribe to it. But look you: it was the naked thing the Walking Woman grasped, not dressed and tricked out, for instance, by prejudices in favor of certain occupations; and love, man love, taken as it came, not picked over and rejected if it carried no obligation of permanancy; and a child; *any* way you get it, a child is good to have, say Nature and the Walking Woman; to have it.

In "The Walking Woman," as in "The Woman at the Eighteen-Mile" and other stories in *Lost Borders*, Mrs. Austin's emotional and political sympathies with the Feminist Movement obviously influence her view of character, though they do not control it. Further, though she praises the Walking Woman's reduction of life's values to "the naked thing" — freedom of feeling and action — she is neither a patent naturalist nor a moralist. She does not suggest the Walking Woman's private revelation as a simple solution; therefore the last lines of the story appropriately leave us with the ambiguity that began it. The author watches the Walking Woman "far down the dim, hot valley....She had a queer, sidelong gait, as if in fact she had a twist all through her....Recollecting suddenly that people called her lame, I ran down to the open place below the spring where she had passed. There in the bare, hot sand the track of her two feet bore evenly and white."

1. Henry Nash Smith, "The Feel of the Purposeful Earth: Mary Austin's Prophecy," *New Mexico Quarterly*, 1931.

2. Mary Austin, *Earth Horizon*, New York, 1932, p. 215.

3. *Ibid.*, p. 216.

Style in the Literary Desert:
Little Big Man

"Doggone it," said Monte, rallying, grinning, "You're prettier'n ever, Miss Hazel, when you get riled that way."

"Riled?" snorted Miss Hazel, sniffing again. "Well, I just never."

Trite? Yes. The same western sounds — "riled," "doggone," "Well, I never."

Out of a third rate pulp or paperback selection? A B-grade Western? Out of *Monte Walsh*, a first rate, major western novel by Jack Schaefer, one of the West's most serious living authors. Page 308. Is this how cowboys and town girls talked to each other in 1887? Probably. It might be argued, with effect, that realism requires authentic dialect, vocabulary, and syntax. Certainly, to judge by the rhetoric colloquially current throughout the West, this sort of conversation makes perfect sense, and should do well for an authentic story out of the West. Yet the triteness will not be wrung from it; the triteness is ingrained. It actually does not matter whether ten thousand cowboys over fifty years regularly used "doggone it" to express a mild surprise or disappointment. The phrase, by this time, has lost its meaning and has no manner. *Realism is at best a limited principle for any artist attempting reality.* The western writer has been dominated by a shallow understanding of the requirements of realism, just as he has been dominated by a shallow understanding of the meaning of narrative.

To get at the cowboy, the western writer will have to
provide him a new speech, as well as a new moral dimension.
Familiarity has bred contempt, and overuse has bred artifici-
ality. The real cowboy, like the real soldier or the real
archbishop, does not require fiction to announce him; history
can do that. He requires interpretation. The bits and pieces of
his reality must be re-sorted. To tell his story for our
imaginations, the western author must travel far beyond
realism, for realism is merely the frontier. Frontiers settle
nothing; they are by definition raw; in art, the raw materials.

Paradoxically, despite all the talk about western formula,
western subjects are unformulated. Jack Schaefer's *Monte
Walsh* is a case in point; and when set off against another
western novel, issued just a year earlier, it becomes a classic
case in point. While Monte Walsh "doggones" it through the
western decades, another kind of hero, Jack Crabb, wagons,
weasles, and wins his way across the four hundred and fifty
pages of *Little Big Man,* one of the finest western novels yet
published. This is an impertinent claim for the 1964 book by
Thomas Berger because it has undeniable faults – it is too long
and episodic. Some will challenge the claim because Berger is a
Midwesterner, not a Westerner; his first two novels, *Crazy in
Berlin* and *Reinhart in Love* are set in Germany and Ohio. But
if Berger were a westerner, he could never have written *Little
Big Man.*

It is satire and incongruity which strike the reader about
this book, especially because both are so seldom used as
important style devices in western writing. Berger has Jack
Crabb tell (into a tape recorder when he is over 100) what
happened to him from 1852 to 1876. Jack is captured by
Indians after part of his family's wagon train is hideously and
hilariously massacred by a small party of Northern Cheyennes.
He lives for some years as the adopted son of Old Lodge Skins,
the chief of a small Northern Cheyenne band. At the
Solomon's Fork battle in 1857, "the first real engagement
between the Army and the Cheyenne," Crabb double-crosses
his adopted people to save his life, and is taken in by a

minister, Pendrake, whose wife Lucy teaches him manners, much as Huckleberry Finn unwillingly learned from the Widow Douglas. He falls in love with Lucy, graduates from this puppy love "to the whores," and finally takes off, leaving the Pendrakes a note: "I can't get onto your ways, though I know they is the right ones." He "goes for gold," with a stopover in brawling St. Louis where he hires himself on as a wagoner to Santa Fe. Raided by Comanches, he resorts to a trick and is captured, escapes to seek shelter at an adobe cabin. "Anybody to home?" he asks, and a short, bandylegged figure answers, "Git on out of here, you hairy son of a whore." He finds out this was Kit Carson: so much for the first of the great western heroes Crabb meets. In Santa Fe he lives with a Mexican woman and her kids, "very morally low at this time, and just sixteen." He falls in with a gold seeker and ends up after a time as a teamster again. After a couple of years of such wandering, his wagon train is raided by the Cheyennes; he ends up back in Old Lodge Skins' camp forgiven and re-adopted. He is not with the Cheyenne in 1864 when Colonel Chivington massacres them at Sand Creek, but he is back with them in 1868 when Custer leads the massacre at the Washita River.

Such is the picaresque pattern of the first half of the novel, which is sometimes too involved and too fragmentary. In these and later wanderings Jack Crabb becomes friends (or enemies) with such trustworthy Western legendmen as Wild Bill Hickok, Wyatt Earp, and George Armstrong Custer. He makes and loses small fortunes, meets and loses and meets again his lunatic sister and good-for-nothing brother; takes a white wife, has a baby by her, loses her; then an Indian wife, then a number of her relatives. He is a bounder, gold miner, gambler, gun-slinger, speculator, sharper, laborer, teamster, buffalo hunter, and finally an unwanted scout for General Custer in the Little Big Horn campaign. This entirely "western," lawless, reckless, and shiftless career is climaxed when Crabb is the only *true* survivor of the Battle of the Little Big Horn, and "If you don't believe it" as he says, "go find another." He is rescued by

Younger Bear, a Cheyenne "brother" who owes him a life-saving obligation.

One of the astonishing qualities of *Little Big Man* is that what happens is much less important than what Crabb, its "central intelligence," makes of his experience: a grand and sad comedy of western manners. Like Huck Finn, Jack Crabb's half-baked education leaves him just literate enough to read signs but intuitive enough to cut through people's appearance. Berger has written that Crabb was "born in my intuition, not my reason," and it is this combination of intuition and reason — in author and character — which makes Crabb a unique western literary creation. Incongruity is the key to humor, and as one would expect in a comedy of manners, the language in *Little Big Man* is an incongruous combination of antithesis, hyperbole, understatement, reversal, irony, and slang. A western backslider aware of irony? A discerning intelligence that continually uses "son of a bitch" and "ain't" to perfection? In Jack Crabb at long last we have the western character who is much more than "Western": Berger's major accomplishment is to treat western materials as part of the greater literary tradition from which they are usually separated.

Jack Crabb's language is both down-to-earth and drawing room, a free-wheeling combination of the vernacular and the literary. After the battle at the Washita, caught between the marauding cavalry and the retreating Indians, Crabb says that "Circumstances seem to disintegrate upon me shortly after I had got settled in them." A little later, having scrambled into a dead cavalryman's uniform, he says, "My feet had room to tour independently within my boots." Traditional western language is either "realistic," as in flat descriptions of massacres; or romantic, as in round, trite descriptions of sunsets. Crabb speaks as of course he would never have spoken — words like "colloquy" and "institution" mingled with "hoss" and "crap" — but this mixture opens the tall tale tradition up to whole new worlds of ideas and fancy by appealing to intellect and imagination at the same time. The mixture is no more outrageous and almost as successful as the best river passages in *Huckleberry Finn;* for instance, Jack Crabb's picture of Wild Bill Hickok, whom he has just outsmarted:

> "Hoss," Hickok says, "you are the trickiest little devil I have ever run across. You know there are a couple of hundred men who would give all they owned to get a clear shot at Wild Bill Hickok, and you throw it away."

> He was laughing, but I reckon somewhere deep he was actually offended, such was his idea of himself. He would rather I had killed him than take pains to show I was basically indifferent to the fact of his existence....

In another scene with Wild Bill, Crabb says of sneaking a glance at a discard in poker, "The practice was frowned on to the degree that if you was caught at it, you could get your head blown off." Berger habitually understates western violence, as when some Cheyennes "got down and pulled Black's body out, stripped him, throwed a lariat over his head and pulled him around the prairie back of a pony until he came apart." He also uses antithesis as when Crabb's Indian wife Sunshine slaps her new baby into consciousness, and Crabb says, "That was also the first and last slap he would ever get from his own kind while moving into a life that otherwise would know every type of mayhem."

Besides language, the characterization is unusually complex in *Little Big Man* and this is doubly important because the three most fully developed characters — Jack Crabb, Old Lodge Skins, and Colonel Custer — represent three of the most overblown types in western fiction: the western hero, the wild Indian, and the cavalryman. Crabb's "father," Old Lodge Skins, is both wise and savage, mystical and foolish, courageous and stoical. He is absolutely *the* "Indian chief" (complete with body odor, multiple wives, peace pipe, and craggy face) and the universal old man who, in another time and place, might have handled parliaments.

In a letter to the author, Berger stated that "*Little Big Man* is a novel and not a western at all, its values those of fiction rather than those of history or other social disciplines." Only by approaching familiar western materials in the novelist's manner — as literature, not as myth, epic, or social drama — could Berger have made George Armstrong Custer compassionate but odious, brilliant but vain, impatient but magnanimous, rational but cruel; in short, a splendid set of human paradoxes. Custer emerges an Elizabethan who might well have carried a show at the Globe. Most important of all, he is a human being, not a tinned military saint or a leaden military villain. At one point, Crabb notices that Custer is getting bald; by such brief but telling little revelations, Berger makes Jack Crabb piece together a new kind of Custer legend, and for the first time Custer really does become a valuable symbol of the western past.

In *Little Big Man,* Berger widens the possibilities of the western novel by treating the Indian-white conflict without melodrama. His view of this conflict is compassionate but realistic, and he never loses sight of the fact that it was both inevitable and two-sided. The sections of *Little Big Man* dealing with the Indian are the most exciting in the book, perhaps because this is the true novelist's ultimate western subject. Readers follow Crabb back into white territory with a sense of loss, for it is among the Cheyenne that Jack himself feels "whole." It is while living in Old Lodge Skins' tepee that Jack comes to understand the ironies and paradoxes of white and Indian world views. To understand *Little Big Man,* then, we must go back to its Indians. When Crabb tells us what they think, say, or do, he speaks from the inside. Perhaps this more than anything else accounts for Berger's success in creating human Indians. Though Crabb may make fun of particular Cheyenne manners, he clearly respects the Cheyenne manner of life; and when he can't stand the society of the Pendrakes in Missouri, he says that "What I had in mind on leaving the Pendrakes was of course returning to the Cheyenne."

From the beginning, Jack's relations with the Cheyenne are a mixture of superstition, magic, misunderstanding, nonsense, and perfect sense. When the wagon party is stopped,

Jack's father and a friend make the "terrible mistake" of trying to buy friendship by giving the Indians whiskey. Immediately drunk, the Cheyennes begin killing both whites and each other — the latter a variation on traditional massacre scenes. They decide to rape the white women, "and if you think there was outcry on the part of the victims, you are wrong" — a turnabout on the classic depredation scene with its shrieking pioneer women. Then, for further incongruity, "those who were not raped stood watching those who were as if waiting their own turn, their children clustered around them." As the scene thickens, Crabb tells us "That left me, with my wet pants —" and the sudden ludicrous, childish touch is unforgettable. When one Cheyenne approaches Crabb's mother, the boy notices that the Cheyenne's face "was not wearing what you generally think of as a cruel or indecent expression but rather one kind of dreamy and genial, like he had every O.K. for his lust."

Sister Caroline saves her mother by knocking the Cheyenne over with a whiplash and then, strangely enough, Old Lodge Skins pointing to the body, "flopped onto his back with his arms crucified and laughed his old mouth, dark as a cave full of bats, into the sun" — a sample of well-structured hyperbole.

The Cheyenne leave and the pioneers bury their dead. Then Old Lodge Skins and two braves return, leading four riderless horses. Sister Caroline, somewhat crazily believing that Old Lodge Skins has fallen for her, says that they have returned to take her away and leave the horses as compensation. This is one of the many misunderstandings that give the book its strange hilarity. As Jack Crabb finds out later, Old Lodge Skins actually brought the horses to make up for the murdered pioneers, and Caroline was only able to force herself and Jack on the Cheyennes because Old Lodge Skins thought she had supernatural powers.

Right from the beginning, Berger makes Indian "superstition" work in the novel. Old Lodge Skins "at last decided we was demons and only waiting for the dark to steal the wits from his head; and while riding along he muttered prayers and incantations to bring us bad medicine." But the only animal that appeared in answer to Old Lodge Skins' prayer was the jackrabbit, "who had a grudge against him of long standing because he once had kept a prairie fire off his camp by exhorting it to burn up the hare's home instead." Crabb goes on, innocently, "I'll say this: I never in my life saw more examples of that animal than when in the company of Old Lodge Skins. Let the toe of his moccasin protrude from the tepee, and up they'd leap for miles around, numerous as sparks when you throw a horseshoe in the forge."

Superstition, or a totally different world view? Crabb says that the Indian doesn't think of time as whites do, "because he ain't, in the white sense, ever going anywhere." He "computes" another way, by his senses:

> Now, looking at a patch of earth, an Indian would see which animals had stopped there during the past two weeks, what birds had flown overhead, and how far it was to the nearest water — this in addition to a lot of supernatural stuff because he does not separate the various types of vitality one from the next.

The practical meaning of the Indian world view has to be dramatized if the reader is to accept it, and in the journey from wagon train to village it is. Old Lodge Skins has sat apparently "in a coma," suddenly to point to a rise. One of the braves strips for action, climbs over, they hear arrows thudding into an animal, and when they all top the rise they find a dead pronghorn antelope. Old Lodge Skins has that uncanny combination of sense perception and intuition which the Indians consider a divine gift. Crabb says, "Old Lodge Skins had detected the beasts on the other side of the hill, though there was no way he could have seen them....The way he knew was having dreamed it."

We know from studies that the Indian has always put great faith in the trance. Soon after arriving at camp, Crabb witnesses an antelope hunt led by Old Lodge Skins. This hunt is the finest piece of set writing in *Little Big Man,* partly because it is not a hunt in the usual sense: the antelope are lured into a living trap of braves, squaws, children, and hounds. Old Lodge Skins had dreamed of antelope the first night Jack was in the village, then gone in a trance by himself to meditate in a small tepee. Braves beat on the tepee's skins till finally Old Lodge Skins emerged with "two short black poles, each with a hoop on its end and decorated with raven feathers." He looked different in that "his eyes seemed to be focused miles away in whatever direction he turned." The nosy antelope would be fatally attracted to the whirling raven feather discs. But, says Crabb, "Admitting that, there was still a lot to a surround that made no sense except as magic." The point is that to Crabb and his readers what then happens does make sense because it is effective magic. Old Lodge Skins sits down at an apparently arbitrary point on the plain, motioning two fat girls to sit beside him. Two thinner girls run with the wheeled pennants and are overtaken by two braves on horses who then carry the pennants over the edge of the low rise in a wide V fanning out from Old Lodge Skins. One antelope, a "Scout," peeks over the top, is curious about the whirling feathers to each side of him, and advances, to be followed by the herd, "placing each dainty hoof as if it was a separate decision." As the herd approaches Old Lodge Skins, "Cheyenne and animals were harmonizing in a grand rhythm, for which the old chief beat time." The riders cross each other behind the herd and ride back, so that "There was now a magic line tied round the antelope, and with a wand in each hand, the chief began to draw it in." Old Lodge Skins seems to be performing a miracle, first in divining that the herd would be just over the ridge, and then in luring the herd to slaughter, while Crabb seems to be saying, "Of course you won't believe this and I tried not to — but it happened; and by God, why not? Jesus did the same." Such hunts are usually presented only as dogged, gruesome, howling, barbaric; but this one has all the order of a quadrille. This is incongruity at its best, and it is not without a touch of mystery.

The incongruity and mystery of Berger's Indians are

clearest in their education of Jack Crabb. The tone in which Crabb tells of it is a happy and unusual combination of wit and circumstance. "It ain't bad to be a boy among the Cheyenne. You never get whipped for doing wrong, but rather told,'This is not the way of the Human Beings.'" Many times Crabb points out that the Indian was more "civilized" in his child rearing and friendships than the white; though Berger takes care never to have Crabb sound sanctimonious. Crabb tells us that one of his young friends, Coyote, once "started to laugh while he was lighting his father's pipe, because a horsefly was crawling on his belly." He then observes, "This was a serious failure of manners...comparable to a white boy's farting in church." By this incongruous analogy, Berger has Crabb impress us with the human value of the education he got. The father's discipline was to say to Coyote, "On account of your lack of self-control I can't smoke all day without disgusting certain Persons in the other world." Crabb's Indian education was based on a universal kind of common sense. He learned mainly by imitating the kids who in turn were imitating their elders. He learned "manners," the social norms and the personal bearing expected of the ideal Cheyenne.

Berger compounded the difficult job of presenting the Indian and white worlds at war by setting Jack Crabb in the thick of the two most famous battles: the Battle of the Washita in 1868 and the Battle of the Little Big Horn in 1876. How do you make something new out of the Washita episode, which has been described in every biography of Custer, in every narrative of the Plains Wars, in every history of the Oklahoma Indian Territory? You do it by re-creating it from an entirely fresh point of view, the Indian's. Crabb tells us that on that fateful morning in November,

> my pony, tethered near, was stirring for a morning drink. Actually — you won't believe this — he looked at me out of his big clear eyes and said: "Father, take me down to the water." I don't mean he spoke in words, but he said it. Then he said: "We are in for a big fight." To hell with what you believe. He said it. I was there.

The tone is now set for a combination of grisly realism and high incongruity which will carry Custer's men through the Indian encampment without violating the evidence of history. Berger is accurate right up to telling us that Custer's men charged to his regimental song "Garry Owen," and that Major Elliott's small command was wiped out downriver. In the midst of mayhem and slaughter, Crabb decides that he must assure the safety of Old Lodge Skins, who was blinded four years before at the Sand Creek massacre. He rushes into the tepee, but the Old man merely says, "My son, sit down beside me and we will smoke." This is not only absurd but splendid, for Old Lodge Skins defends his refusal to budge with a kind of logic which by this time we have come to accept: "I am blind and cannot fight. Yet neither will I run. If it is my day to die, I want to do it here, within a circle." Old Lodge Skins has that stoicism about death which the Indian has so often coupled with aggressiveness in mortal combat. Despite his Cheyenne years and training, Crabb's "whiteness" makes this suggestion seem outrageous, and he tries unsuccessfully to knock the old man out so he can drag him to the river. Finally, he gives up and lights the pipe:

> He puffed on the pipe and offered the usual smoke clouds to East and West, etc. By God, I thought, he is sticking to it, he is an Indian to the core. You know how you think about foreigners, savages and so on, that in an emergency they'll be just like yourself, even to talking English. But it was me who had to become Cheyenne here.

Promptly, Jack offers a prayer to the White Buffalo Spirit. Then Old Lodge Skins sights an intruding soldier "on sound," and shoots him out of the tepee entrance with his double muzzle-loader. Having made war, he agrees to consider escape, but this requires finding his wampum bag and his war bonnet. Crabb tells us that a wampum bag usually contains "a handful of feathers, the foot of an owl, a deerbone whistle, the dried pecker of a buffalo, and suchlike trash." Old Lodge Skins wants to show Jack the war bonnet, and insists on Jack's getting "his sacred bow and quiver of arrows, and then a special blanket, and of course his powder horn and shot bag, and his pipe and tobacco case." Jack complains, "I'm loaded down with this crap, and the United States Cavalry is blowing out the front of the lodge." Suddenly, after putting on "bracelets, bear-claw necklaces, breastplate of tiny bones and the lot," Old Lodge Skins says "Come, my son. We cannot stay in this tepee all day. The soldiers are about to burn it down." They cross the battlefield unharmed.

How can we account for the behavior of the old man during one of the bloodiest massacres on record? We can't, and we needn't try. This scene is no more meant literally than much of the business in *Don Quixote*, with which at times *Little Big Man* may be compared. The Indian Wars were logically and politically absurd. The Army outnumbered the Indians in nearly every engagement, yet had to fight a hundred-year European war. On the other side, the Indian refused to submit to the inevitable even after such massacres as those at Sand Creek and the Washita. Underneath all was the one factor, the utter difference in world view, which guaranteed the carnage. This is what Berger brings to life in Old Lodge Skins' ceremonial response to what was, in itself, a traditional ritual of mass slaughter. Old Lodge Skins appeals to us as the self-respecting center of a meaningless, turning western, American world. This difference in world view is brought to a lyrical climax in the final scene of the book, after Crabb's rescue from Custer's Last Stand, when Old Lodge Skins climbs to timberline in the Big Horn Mountains to die. Jack, the only "son" left alive, goes with him, and tells us that the sky was "real pale blue...like a dome made of sapphire....If you was a bird you could keep going straight up forever, fast as you could fly, yet you would always be in the same place." Such sharp imagery controls the presentation of vast western nature in this entire scene, and that nature seems to be compressed into a wizened old chief about to die. Berger's admission that he wept when he wrote this scene is easy to believe, for by the time Old Lodge Skins blasts out his great Cheyenne war cry, defying Death to "Come out and fight!'' we do not want the old man to die — he is too valuable and universal. Begun as a character in a novel, he has become myth. Now he prays to the Everywhere Spirit, "Thank you for making me a Human Being [a Cheyenne] !...Thank you for all my victories and for all my defeats. Thank you for my vision, and for the blindness in which I saw further." As he chants, the crystal sky quickly becomes great clouds, and rain falls. He makes a last request, "Take care of my son here, and see that he does not go crazy," then simply lays down and dies. There is not a word of sentimentality in the entire scene.

Little Big Man is a significant novel because it portrays western "society" in the nineteenth century as it really was — violent, yes, but also absurd, melodramatic, incongruous. Its author never sacrifices his imagination to realism. At the same time it is scrupulously accurate as to places, dates and events, the results of the "60 or 70 accounts of the Western reality" which Berger says he read "to reinforce my feeling for the myth." It is also "the Western to end all Westerns" which Berger intended it to be, because it splendorizes the West with love and imagination. Far from discarding any of the choice western properties, Berger has turned them inside out, revealing one by one the possibilities of a western literary art.

The Possibility of a Western Poetics

"and I am waiting
for the discovery
of a new symbolic western frontier"

(Lawrence Ferlinghetti)

We have plenty of Western American verse, but little poetry — and no poetics. We have no attitudes by which poets can discipline their imaginative responses to the West's landscape, history, folklore, language, or simply its humanity. From before Bret Harte till after John Neihardt, western verse has lacked wit, irony, paradox, metaphor, or symbol. Instead, it has been a single dimension response to a giant landscape and a noisy history. Excepting Thomas Hornsby Ferril and Yvor Winters, the consciously "western poet" has not attempted to transmute this landscape, or its history, into troubling emotion or complex idea. As a cause, and as a result, western poetry is without literary criticism.

By "western" I mean the area beginning in those Great Plains lands originally taken over for cattle grazing and extending to the Pacific Coast. It is possible to consider the *agricultural* settlement of the Plains as distinctly "Midwestern" because agrarian settlement dominated Midwestern patterns, but was relatively unimportant West of the One-Hundredth Meridian. Most commentators have thought of the West as "a form of society," in Frederick Jackson Turner's phrase. They have exaggerated its uniqueness on the basis of physical grandeur, bonanza economies, and lawlessness. They have both deduced and invented character-types like the "bloodthirsty Indian," the gold miner, the carefree cowboy, the loner mountain man and the laconic gunslinger as lawless but godfearing, violent but pious, ignorant but ingenious; but the meaning of such paradoxes has seldom interested western thinkers and writers. Fortunes have regularly been made by ignoring them. Western verse, in particular, has been written from an oversimplified perspective and in an oversimplified manner.

Thus the big sky, the long plains, the giant trees, the panoramic sunsets, the prance-pony cavalry officer, the gutsy sodbuster, the wild mining camp, and the psychotic gunslinger have been romanticized in regular meter and rhyme. They have been versified almost as often as fictionalized, though most of these stanzas have thankfully disappeared in unread old newspapers and out-of-print periodicals and brochures.

Two western versifiers did become both prominent and influential after the sudden bonanza in California began. In Joaquin Miller's *Songs of the Sierras* and in Bret Harte's *East and West Poems* we have a permanent record of the western poetry read widely in the last century and still copied regionally today. The volumes were published in 1870 and 1871 respectively, but many of the poems they contained had been published in the previous decade. The verses abound in ballad narrative, local color, and ballooning nature description. Moreover, despite the fact that naturalism, symbolism, imagism, and New Criticism subsequently revolutionized poetic expression elsewhere, most western verse continues to be written at the level of Bret Harte's "The Society upon the Stanislaus." Nearly everyone knows Truthful James, who tells "in simple language what I know about the row/ That broke up our Society upon the Stanislow." The narrative has to do with a hoax which led to a "row":

> Then Abner Dean of Angel's raised a point of order, when
> A chunk of old red sandstone took him in the abdomen,
> And he smiled a kind of sickly smile, and curled up on
>   the floor

And the subsequent proceedings interested him no more.

There is little difference in subject or style in the following poem, written early in this century by a man who worked in western mines:

> Hearing them knocking — listen — there!
> Ghosts of miners — fighting for air.
> Faint — far away — down the slope —
> Picking the cave in — and no hope.
> You hear them knocking in the Elm Orlu,
> In Leadville mines, and at Granite, too —
> In the Coeur d'Alenes, and the Comstock Lodes,
> And in soft coal mines, where gas explodes —
> Hear them! Listen — quiet — there!
> Ghosts of miners — wanting air.

The major difference between the two poems is their time perspective. The poet who hears miners' ghosts knocking in abandoned shafts is trying to recapture the spirit of mining times, while Harte was presenting that spirit to contemporary audiences. Harte's mood is topical while the later poet's is nostalgic, and the verse quality is similarly limited by trite rhyming, intrusive rhythm, topical reference, and lack of idea.

Granted that the line between "verse" and "poetry" is difficult to draw, we must still draw it to make sense of the western application. I think "verse" is formally organized expression distinguishable from prose by compressed arrangements of rhythm and, usually, of rhyme; I think "poetry" is verse elevated by the *quality* of compression. Perhaps "quality" may be defined as imaginative reach. When I say that we have no western poetics, I mean that we lack the literary techniques and the literary theories that must reinforce these techniques, for expressing the West with imaginative reach. The term "poetics" has many dictionary definitions, but they cross each other at the key word "poem," and they all include the idea of poetic theory. In order to emphasize the lack of a western poetics I have purposely chosen, above, two poems anthologized in the 1932 edition of *Western Prose and Poetry* by Rufus Coleman. His preface remarks tell us something important about the traditional purposes of western writers. Noting first that the West has been judged "by its worst writing," he praises the "increasing body of authentic narrative" and suggests that his collection may be read as social history. He tells us that he has arranged the material chronologically "in an effort to fit into their proper places many of the striking events of this great moving picture of the West." Very much in western tradition, the ingredients of art are those of history and entertainment, emphasizing the panoramic, the narrative, and the topical. Thus western writers record and recreate the apparent actual, with regional dialect, customs, and events. As Coleman wrote, "Some of the narratives are wild but not woolly — at least not objectionably so. The fleece, at all events, is of good length and texture."

Certainly authenticity is a step in the right direction. By placing a higher value on actual situations and believable characters recent western writers such as Walter Van Tilburg Clark and A. B. Guthrie, Jr., have brought Western fiction into the twentieth century. By separating history and legend, recent commentators such as Floyd Steckmesser and Rodman Paul have given both history and legend new dignity. They have recognized that the "civilizing" process is a strengthening one, and they have helped to mature western comment. Yet, as I shall try to show, there has not been such a maturing in western poetry; there has been little intention of art. Whereas recent novelists and short story writers *have* seemed to agree informally that style must at last be planted in the desert, the poets seem informally agreed not to consider whether free verse, the lyric, symbolism, esthetic distance, or the submerged metaphor can have western poetic meaning. Most western poetry still reads like last century's parlor wall illustrations. Consider the typical example by Edwin Markham which faces the title page in *Western Prose and Poetry:*

> Now, sons of the West, I see you rise,
> The world's young courage in your eyes.

Sons of broad-shouldered Pioneers,
Seasoned by struggle and stern tears—....

Build greatly, men, for she must shine
With Athens of the singing Nine—....

Here is all the romanticism which flowered vulgarly in the
architecture and place names of nineteenth century America:
Achilles in mine shafts and Ulysses on mountain trails.

Even better poets than Markham have been unable to bring
their best to the West. Consider these lines from Carl
Sandburg's "Slabs of the Sunburnt West":

Panels of the cold gray open night,
Gates of the Great American Desert,
    Skies keeping the prayers of the wagon men,
    The riders with picks, shovels and guns,
On the old trail, the Santa Fe Trail, the Raton Pass
Panels, skies, gates, listen tonight while we send up our
    prayers on the Santa Fe Trail.

The flat adjective sequence in the first line typically suggests
the imaginative plateau of western poetry. "Night" has no
particular or unusual quality; nor does the cliché "riders,"
presented wholly as a thousand costumed movie pioneers. As
in most western verse, the only allusions are to famous place
names (or hero names) to stimulate some kind of myth-gut
response. The "picks, shovels and guns" of the wagon men
have no particularity. They are topically listed familiar
artifacts of settlement; thus the poem is simply a report. Is this
limitation Sandburg's? His ability to transmute familiar objects
into imaginative poetry, for instance in "Prayers of Steel,"
suggests that the limitation is in the tradition, not the poet.

Sandburg and Markham both write in debt to Whitman,
though most "folk" poets seem to reflect only part of what
Whitman himself intended. By and large, their western verse
only compares to what we call "bad Whitman." In *Democratic
Vistas,* Whitman predicted that "In a few years the dominion-

heart of America will be far inland, toward the West." He
believed that the Ohio, Mississippi, and Missouri River regions
("spine-character of the States") would "compact and settle
the traits of America." From the West, "solid personality, with
blood and brawn," Whitman constructed a romantic poetic
subject, then asked why we did not find "the Mississippi,
stalwart western man, real mental and physical facts,
Southerners, etc., in the body of our literature? especially the
poetic part of it?" But if blood, brawn, and real mental and
physical facts had been the only substance of Whitman's
poetics for America or for the West, he would never have
written "Out of the Cradle Endlessly Rocking," "I Saw in
Louisiana a Live-Oak Growing," "Song of Myself," or the
other masterpieces we prefer to separate as "great Whitman."
Inchoate though his poetry theory was, it took into account
the complexity necessary for any important poetic expression.
Like the critical-minded of his time, Whitman did insist upon
the importance of intellection and tradition, not just of folk
emotion and the vernacular. He also said in *Democratic Vistas,*
"But woe to the age or land in which these things, movements,
stopping at themselves, do not tend to ideas." He told us he
had found "such ideas" in Homer, "the sacred bards of
Jewry," Aeschylus, Juvenal, and Shakespeare. Apparently
Whitman had in mind a poetics and a poetry which could
make of the West, as of the "divine American aggregate," a
complex mystical expression, not just a courageously concrete
one.

To a degree the failure of any poet to make matter of
western materials resulted from Whitman's own failure, as a
critic, to give poets a concrete, detailed set of principles and
practices — that is, a formalized poetics. The best he did was
to demonstrate in his best work (never of or about the western
half of the country) what could be done. All his attempts to
rhapsodize the West are comparative failures. The best-known
is "Pioneers! O Pioneers!":

> Come my tan-faced children,
> Follow well in order, get your weapons ready,

> Have you your pistols? have you your sharp-edged axes?
>   Pioneers! O pioneers!...
>
>   O you youths, Western youths,
> So impatient, full of action, full of manly pride and
>   friendship
> Plain I see you Western youths, see you tramping with
>   the foremost
>   Pioneers! O pioneers!...

In twenty-six such stanzas Whitman manages to invoke nearly every familiar western cliché: a rhythmic moving picture of the West. An even longer poem, "The Song of the Redwood Tree," is probably the least effective of his song cycle.

While Whitman never succeeded out West, his other successes point out the need for western poets to suffuse stark concreteness with the quality of mystery, and thereby to make familiar materials into something new. This is not the place to discuss such a masterwork as "Song of Myself," except to point out that the overwhelming physicality of its rhythms, images, and topics resembles the stark realism upon which western writers seem to be insisting in their materials. Whereas "Song of Myself" soars without inhibition, western writer's verses are ground-bound by their insistence on "authenticity" and folk ballad cadence.

Neither Whitman nor Sandburg is a western poet, but the fully western credentials of John Neihardt cannot be questioned. Here is a better-than-average sample of his technique, taken from the same western "reality" as "Slabs of the Sun-Burnt West" and "Pioneers! O Pioneers!" — movement along the trails:

>   He struck a trot,
>   Eyes fixed upon the trail. The sun rose hot;
>   Noon poured a blinding glare upon the draws;
>   And still the trail led on, without a pause
>   To show where Mike had rested. Thirst began
>   To be a burden on the little man...

As in so many passages in *A Cycle of the West,* this one bulges with trite phrases depicting only physical movement: "struck a trot," "eyes fixed upon the trail," "the sun rose hot," "the trail led on." It might almost be said that movement is the curse of western verse, for its writers never pause long enough to reflect on the nature of the nature through which their heroes trot.

Such criticism is open to the counter-argument that the history of the West is a history of movement — of violent action in a giant landscape. Yet it is this very kind of reasoning which most conclusively proves the absence of, and the need for, a western poetics. It is not the business of poetry merely to retell history or to abbreviate the descriptions of naturalists, government surveyors, or diarists: the province of poetry is the human consciousness, as Whitman's best poetry suggested.

Perhaps, as a byproduct of broader interests, a faint beginning has been made toward a western poetics. It may seem odd at first that this much-needed pioneering has been done by eastern and midwestern poets, but considering that a poetics must be grounded in traditions, the geographical displacement is logical. It seems clear that if such a poetics is ever to be developed the stimulus must continue to be eastern until writers from the Rocky Mountains, the Great Basin, and the Sierras are willing to set aside topical and descriptive complacency. The difference between all the verse I have discussed so far, and poetry, can quickly be sensed in E. E. Cumming's "tribute":

> Buffalo Bill's
> defunct
>   who used to
>   ride a watersmooth-silver
>   stallion
>   and break onetwothreefourfive pigeons just like that
>   Jesus
> he was a handsome man
>   and what i want to know is

how do you like your blueeyed boy
Mister Death

Perhaps the first critical difference is in purpose. Whitman, Sandburg and Neihardt were "singing" the "saga" of settlement (I am using Neihardt's words) while Cummings was satirizing the hoax aspects of that settlement. This poem has been interpreted as complimentary to Buffalo Bill's splendor, but I believe its satiric intent is set in the second line by the word "defunct," which connotes "good and thankfully dead." The image "blueeyed boy" suggests the Anglo-Saxon absurdity behind such western-isms as Manifest Destiny and the frontier hypothesis. We do not need words such as "gun," "pistol," "shooting iron" or "six shooter" to appreciate the satire of breaking "onetwothreefourfive [shooting gallery] pigeons just like that." In less than a dozen lines the western hero has been unhorsed, and at least one very serious question about the nature of our exalted frontier has been suggested. Cummings achieves all this, as it must be achieved for the West, by a severe abstraction of details, by leaving out, rather than in. He intensifies meaning by stripping imagery, and his meaning is critical, interpretive.

Still it might be argued that a narrative intent requires the rambling, descriptive techniques of most western versemakers. As the narratives of Whitman, T.S. Eliot, Hart Crane and Robert Frost show, intensity is not dependent on brevity, nor is depth a necessary casualty of scope. "Song of Myself" is long, digressive, even epic-like. It is also figuratively intense. It works on the imagination, from the imagination. Yet the purpose behind "Song of Myself," as spelled out in the 1855 Preface to *Leaves of Grass,* is similar in many ways to the purpose John Neihardt spells out in his Introduction to *A Cycle of the West:*

> The period with which the Cycle deals was one of discovery, exploration and settlement — a genuine epic period, differing in no essential form from the other great epic periods that marked the advance of the Indo-European peoples out of Asia and across Europe. It was a time of intense individualism, a time

when society was cut loose from its roots....For this reason
only, the word "epic" has been used in connection with the
Cycle; it is properly descriptive of the mood and meaning of the
time and of the material with which I have worked. There has
been no thought of synthetic Iliads and Odysseys, but only of
the richly human saga-stuff of a country that I knew and
loved....

The "intense individualism" and the uniqueness of American
"discovery exploration and settlement" suggest epic as the
"mood and meaning of the time and of the material" in much
the same way that Whitman saw the same pioneer and frontier
features. In "Song of Myself" and the best of *Leaves of Grass,*
Whitman expresses "mood and meaning" in a style that gives
the grand American story a poetic life of its own. Beyond his
thematic purposes, then, what are Neihardt's stylistic intentions? Apparently to suggest an epic quality not in meaning,
and not much in mood, but in movement alone. His characters
generally have no motive beyond physical endurance, or
sometimes a detached personal loyalty. They are only heroes
of action.

Again, it might be argued that it is absurd to force
"motive" on such eventful careers as those of Jed Smith,
Daniel Boone, or Jim Bridger. It is — so long as western poets
are content to distort western history, so that "intense
individualism" is measured by the hero's instinct for survival.
On the other hand, Cummings' little poem has reminded us
that one of the West's patent heroes may also be subjected to
judgment. The implication of Cummings' address to Mister
Death is that the western epic may have been grotesque, after
all.

But satire such as Cummings' is not the only kind of
poetry that nonwesterners have successfully made of western
materials. In "The River" section of *The Bridge,* Hart Crane
has written both rhapsodically and critically about our sacred
western settlement. Though "the river" here is the Mississippi,
the poem qualifies for our discussion because Crane was
interested in the westward movement as continuing "common

man" frontier. Part of Crane's purpose, like Neihardt's, is panoramic; part of his purpose, like Whitman's and Sandburg's, is inspirational. What distinguishes his lines is style. We see this in the difference between Sandburg's description of the westerning train and Crane's:

> Sandburg: Into the night, into the blanket of night,
> Into the night rain gods, the night luck gods,
> Overland goes the overland passenger train.
>
> Crane: Stick your patent name on a signboard
> brother — all over — going West — young man
> Tintex — Japalac — Certain-teed Overalls ads
> and land sakes!...

Crane translates the West in many other exciting ways:

> Yes, turn again and sniff once more — look see,
> O Sheriff, Brakeman and Authority —
> Hitch up your pants, and crunch another quid,
> For you, too, feed the River timelessly....
>
> Down, down — born pioneers in time's despite,
> Grimed tributaries to an ancient flow —
> They win no frontier by their wayward plight,
> But drift in stillness, as from Jordan's brow.

Crane moves heroes from their six-gun confrontations to eternal relations. They can hitch up their pants in country western style, but they will return, beyond their "democratic" moment, into time. In both these stanzas he "heaps" the river upon our imaginations by freshly using familiar frontier and pioneer materials.

Earlier in "The River," to cross imaginatively from the rushing Twentieth Century Limited to the Great Plains it was leaving behind, Crane invokes the West in one of the great passages of American poetry:

> The last bear, shot drinking in the Dakotas,
> Loped under wires that span the mountain stream.
> Keen instruments, strung to a vast precision
> Bind town to town and dream to ticking dream.

> But some men take their liquor slow — and count...
> The river's minute by the far brook's year.
> Under a world of whistles, wires and steam
> Caboose-like they go, ruminating through
> Ohio, Indiana — blind baggage —
> To Cheyenne tagging...Maybe Kalamazoo.

Here is a western past sensitive to our own time. First, the passing of "the old West": "The last bear, shot drinking in the Dakotas," the last region to be settled. Crane seems to bemoan free nature's "fencing" by industrialism. But these lines have more to say, for they suggest both the gains and the losses: the exhilaration *and* the fears that Whitman felt at materialism running wild. This theme tension, basic to *The Bridge,* may suggest to twentieth century poets of the West's nineteenth century one way to make art of history. For there is no question that the travesties as well as the glories acted out beyond the Mississippi foreshadowed the blazing scream of the Twentieth Century Limited across Hart Crane's land.

Technically, how does style work in Crane's use of western materials? First, in disciplined leaving out, rather than piling in, of references. The second line of "The River" has an incredibly western cliche: "going West — young man." We soon learn that we are riding a train west, westering along the old trails — the classic frontier movement. The train is really a mechanized refraction of the covered wagon, but the train swiftly becomes also a symbol, for was it not for this that the pioneers lumbered toward the Rockies and the Sierras? We do not have in this poem the same young man that Horace Greeley intended, and so the allusion has moved far beyond cliché.

Indian idea is also important in "The River," though centered at first in Pocahontas, an easterner:

> Trains sounding the long blizzards out — I heard
> Wail into distances I knew were hers.
> Papooses crying on the long wind's mane
> Screamed redskin dynasties that fled the brain,

> Dead echoes! But I knew her body there,
> Time like a serpent down her shoulder dark,
> And space, an eaglet's wing, laid on her hair.

We have a sense here of both tragedy and timelessness; the death of tribes and ways of life; the mystical continuation of their being through us, their destroyers. The next lines bring the Indian westward, "Under the Ozarks," briefly imaging the Indian creation myth and climaxing in a contrast between the "buried" Indian civilizations and the conquering American one:

> Such pilferings make up their timeless eatage,
> Propitiate them for their timber torn
> By iron, iron — always the iron dealt cleavage!
> They doze now, below axe and powder horn.
>
> And Pullman breakfasters glide glistening steel
> From tunnel into field — iron strides the dew —
> Straddles the hill, a dance of wheel on wheel.

Reading backwards, the pioneer rape ("iron dealt cleavage") and conquest ("iron strides the dew/Straddles the hill") of the "virgin land" are presented as both nineteenth and twentieth century experience. The "rape" is foreshadowed in the earlier stanza, as trains "wail," "papooses" cry, and "redskin dynasties" scream, so that when Crane uses two familiar western artifacts, "axe and powder horn" they mean something new: not only horror, but tragedy.

One of my reasons for discussing "The River" at length is that Crane intended, in his own words, *The Bridge* to be "an epic of the modern consciousness." He wrote during the 1920's, at the same time John Neihardt was developing his *Cycle* as a serial-epic of western exploit. One measure of the difference between verse and poetry is in the juxtaposition of "consciousness" and "exploit." Recently, a number of contemporary poets have shown that the gap can be closed between western verse and poetry. Perhaps the future possibility of a western poetics is best indicated in some of the work that Thomas Hornsby Ferril has been doing for many years in the Rocky Mountains. First, Ferril's sense of history takes him beyond the usual western awe of space to an awareness of time, as in "Nothing Is Long Ago":

> Here in America nothing is long ago:
> George Washington was never in Oregon,
> He never saw a Flathead woman flop
> Her breast across her shoulder to a child,
> He never saw the stranded cedar bark
> Blow from her salmon thighs like a weaver's thrums.
> But it wasn't long:
> The corn came quick enough
> For Buffalo Bill to eat it out of a can
> In a barber shop in a circus tent in London.
> You used to see the old man hanging around
> The City Desk as if it were a bee tree.

It is interesting that Ferril, like Cummings, focuses on Buffalo Bill, though not for satire. What Ferril seems to be expressing is his own sense (a sense any western writer should share) of how much was left behind in the headlong rush. The poet implies a longing for tradition.

All this aside, the poem also has the merit of incongruity, a device of wit practically never used in poems of the West: the corn (of nature) canned for a western hero to eat five thousand miles east, doing horserider stunts for the Old World. Later in the poem, he also uses the device of reversal:

> Nothing is long ago when you hear a saw:
> It cuts so quick the centuries of pitch
> The seasons wrap in rings around a tree....

Though often given to straight description, Ferril sometimes transmutes the physical West, as in "Time of Mountains":

> When you've walked a long time on the floor of a river,
> And up the steps and into the different rooms,
> You know where the hills are going....

The sudden architectural imagery gives new meaning to the familiar canyon pattern through which the riverbed cuts. In fact the earlier line in which the canyon is introduced, "The dark impounded orders of this canyon," has already set the

tone for an unusual combination of image and idea. Again, in
the long and uneven poem, "Words for Leadville," Ferril
sometimes does new things with other materials, as when he
questions the power of time as "A timber thing/ When August
dried the velvet in the antlers/ Of a thousand centuries?" In
"Ghost Town," for all intents and purposes a companion piece,
he does other interesting things with time:

> The things with blossoms take an old house down
> More quietly than wind, more slow than mountains....
>
> And I can hear the mountains falling down
> Like thunder going home.

For a final comment we can do no better than to note a
discussion, "Poetry of the West," by Alan Swallow. First
presented at the 1964 annual conference of the Western
History Association, the paper has both familiar emotional
overtones and unusual critical undertones. Since the Swallow
Press is an oasis of quality, we owe no small homage to its
creator; and since Alan Swallow has written worthy western
poetry as well as published it, he is particularly qualified to
state its case.

At first, the paper seems entirely regional because it seems
entirely topical; as Swallow himself says toward the end, "I see
by now I have lapsed into names." And, too, it has a kind of
emotional hyperbole, a fervid regional loyalism familiar in
descriptions of big sky sunsets. Under this spell, Swallow
asserts that western-settled Yvor Winters and J. V. Cunning-
ham are "the best poets now alive writing in the English
language." He also says that no other region "could match
[western] production in quality for the equivalent time [1920
to present] covered by the active lives of these poets." At the
same time, and with a familiar dismissal of contradictions,
Swallow points out that "the West has been home and
battleground and place of some remarkable creative endeavor,
but not a single 'poetic way of life'." Logically, then, the West
has achieved poetic supremacy without a poetics. This seems

first a paradox and second an exaggeration. Swallow himself states of the western poets who enlivened the twenties, "their themes had largely to be imported; and their methods are imported." Of Winters' western-set poems he says, "these are poems of the vastest themes, learned, inherited, from all of world literature."

While I cannot agree with Swallow's unqualified estimate of Winters' poetry, I can agree that the poet's use of irony, antithesis, and other intensifying means lifts such poems as "California Oaks" and "John Day, Frontiersman" above the workday topicality and flat imagery of most western verse. In the latter poem we read:

> Broken at last by very force of frame,
> By wintry hunger like a warrior's brand,
> You died a madman. And now bears your name
> A gentle river in a fertile land....
>
> The eminence is gone that met your eye;
> The winding savage, too, has sunk away.
> Now, like a summer myth, the meadows lie,
> Deep in the calm of silvan slow decay.

This is clean lyricism, in a classic and pastoral manner. It fairly represents Winters' relation to western poetics and shows that Winters' ideas are not much help in formulating a distinctively western poetics. Swallow points to Winters' formula of clarity in conception, and purity and freedom from mannerism in style, as influential on the best of western poetry. The "school of poets" Swallow claims Winters to have founded is thus seeking intense expression in general esthetic terms. While such traditions of taste, style, and balance are certainly needed, they can only feed into the western tradition. They cannot become it.

It seems that even from his editor's desk Swallow is unable to detect an organized, qualitative, and profoundly western endeavor. The best he can arrive at is a conviction that "the ingredient which might make the West take leadership in

American letters and 'teach' the rest of the nation...a thing or two about writing great poetry, would be rationality." He defines this as "the overall attitude that poetry itself is responsible human behavior." This call to humanistic, critically-centered letters reflects the influence of Yvor Winters. Indeed, I believe that here is the point at which the larger Western world tradition and the individual western American tradition ought to collide, both in library carrels and in baking arroyos.

One stunning example of such possibilities appeared in the September, 1964, issue of *Poetry*. The Plains buffalo has fascinated writers for two centuries, but it has never been treated with the sensitivity and esthetic sense of Thomas McGrath:

> "The Buffalo Coat"
> I see him moving, in his legendary fleece,
> Between the superhighway and the Algonquin stone axe;
> Between the wild tribes in their lost heat
> And the dark blizzard of my Grandfather's coat;
> Cold with the outdoor cold caught in the curls,
> Smelling of the world before the poll tax.
>
> And between the new macadam and the Scalp Act
> They got him by the short hair; had him clipped
> Who once was wild — and all five senses wild —
> Printing the wild with his hoof's inflated script
> Before the times was money in the bank,
> Before it was a crime to be so mild.
>
> But history is a fact, and moves on feet
> Sharper than his, toward wallows deeper than.
> And the myth that covered all his moving parts,
> Grandfather's time had turned into a coat;
> And what kept warm then, in the true world's cold
> Is old and cold in a world his death began.[1]

As in the Ferril poems, time is an instrument of telling here, especially in the "dark blizzard of my Grandfather's coat." By symbolizing the buffalo, many have tried to express their sense of the dying American Indian age. Vachel Lindsay has hymned "The Flower-Fed Buffaloes" and wailed about "The Ghost of the Buffaloes." In folk song, Buffy Sainte Marie has sung "Now That the Buffalo's Gone." To one degree or another, each of these has been limited by nostalgia, controlled by regret. What makes McGrath's poem both different and superior? Partly, his use of antithesis, the classic technique of placing next to each other two wildly different ideas or images, as in "between the new macadam and the Scalp act" or the old coat's "Smelling of the world before the poll tax." The lines are packed with implications suggested by these diversities and contradictions. Implications are impossible without ideas, and the final stanza is a remarkable example of making idea work in verse. Beginning with the generalization that "history is a fact," quickly made concrete as it "moves on feet/ Sharper than his, toward wallows deeper than," the stanza is all idea — and all poetry. The final lines transcribe the passing away of that untamed nature with regret, but also with intense perception of the *feeling* that regret covers: "And what kept warm then, in the true world's cold/ Is old and cold in a world his death began." The lines are saturated with humanity as well as history; they have natural dignity, and a great deal of style.

After reading such a poem it is impossible to believe that the West will not yield to poetry or that a western poetics is a contradiction. Such a poetics can be organized, first, by throwing off esthetic defensiveness, with its foolish corollary insistence that the West is "unique," therefore culturally separable. The poet must take the West seriously so that he can at last regard its materials with critical detachment and intensity. Criticism encourages distance, and poets need such distance to force the imagination's excitement. Imagination, in turn, requires complexity to satisfy itself.

From this kind of distance the western poet will see how

really unimportant "authentic narrative" is and how absolutely important interpretation is, as in Ferril's river bed, no longer static sand through rock canyon; or in McGrath's buffalo coat, no longer threadbare pelt.

However, these both radical and conservative necessities do not preclude an important tradition in the West: humor. In fact, if more recent Hollywood movies are for once a meaningful barometer, the West may become distinguished in a new use of the absurd. *The Hallalujah Trail* and especially *Cat Ballou* have given audiences something they are willing to pay a high week-end price for: a cowboy-cavalryman-gunman West which knows how to laugh at its own absurdities. Cummings' little Buffalo Bill poem and Thomas Berger's novel *Little Big Man* have the same high quality absurdity. Though not apparent, there is an important relationship between the poems of Ferril and McGrath, and these, for they all express the West freshly by using literary traditions freshly. In *Cat Ballou* the hilarious lampoon of the standard gunman in Kid Shaleen had many of the ingredients of classic satire, and Lee Marvin's huge success in that role, excellent as his acting may have been, was due in part to the audiences' instinctive response to the esthetic taste built into the part.

The first and most important step, then, in creating a worthy western poetry will be a conscious attempt by western poets to infuse western tradition with the larger literary traditions. The possibilities are fabulous.

1. Copyright 1964 by Thomas McGrath. Reprinted by permission of *Poetry.*

The West and the New Dissent

Certainly the new dissenter has not declared the West the land of his salvation, nor has he made major heroes out of western heroes. His preference is for spiritual and political leaders such as Buddha, Jesus, Gandhi, Che Guevara, Ho Chi Minh and Malcolm X. The connection between the West and the new dissenter is mainly in the collective unconscious of his counter culture. A counter culture is a set of values, life styles and activities which develop as rejections of the mainstream and as substitutes for it. For example, the hippie seeking detachment is attracted to the physical West because land is less crowded and cheaper, the sky more encompassing, and nature's harmony less disturbed. But this interest in land leads to a heightened sense of the western past and the myths shaped out of it. The new dissenter as political theoretician begins to think about the West while seeking connections between populism and the new people's movements. Consciously, he is learning about farm and labor history in Nebraska or Idaho, unconsciously, he is absorbing western myth, a romanticized version of the past that pervades the mother culture. The western hero at the center of this myth is the inner-directed, free individual, a man of true grit who backs up his convictions with fist and gun. Undertaking full responsibility for himself in a harsh world, he lives out a simple, virile existentialism. But when the new dissenter encounters the real and present West, he discovers the paradox that myth has masked. Invoking the tradition of the free individual, westerners more frequently than any other kind of American wish to suppress the freedom of individuals with whom they disagree. At a time when nationalism seems at least absurd, and more likely evil, the westerner often becomes the superpatriot, the isolationist, or the hard core rightist who believes the United Nations is a communist conspiracy from which the United States must immediately withdraw. The national headquarters of the John Birch Society is in New England; of the Minute Men, in Missouri; but both groups are most active in the West. In recent national elections, the West has led the conservative vote. Despite an occasional maverick such as Frank Church or Wayne Morse, the western trend is to leaders whose political philosophy might be expected to send the new dissenter running.

But he doesn't run. Rather, he relates himself to the West. Why?

First, because all groups require myths and heroes to sustain collective belief. In the words of mythologist Joseph Campbell, the hero is the one "who has been able to battle past his personal, local and historical limitations to the generally valid, normally human forms."[1] We should add that the hero may also be pushed past these limitations by the combined imagination of his society. The hero embodies the values of his people, and celebrates those values in his myth-life. Anthropologist Bronislaw Malinowski says that myth "supplies a retrospective pattern of moral values, sociological order, and magical belief." Myth dramatizes tradition and keeps it fresh through constant magical renewal.[2] In our time, when the realities of life have shattered most American myths, the Western Hero continues to excite belief, both in society at large, and in the counter culture of the new dissenter.

Since change is the only constant in our society, the present counter culture is based on dissent, and cannot be understood in any other way. Despite its importance, this dissent has seldom been clearly defined; the 1967 edition of *The Encyclopedia of the Social Sciences* does not deal with it directly. Let us say dissent is disagreement with an established order, ideally on a moral basis, for the purpose of bringing about change through personal or group action. In politics, the action may consist of letter-writing, demonstrating or disrupting. There are parallel means in scholarship, art, education and social custom. Some believe dissent may include destruction of property, or even life, and others maintain that nonviolence is a *sine qua non* of true dissent. Ideologically, dissent may exist to the left or to the right of the status quo. A radical leftist, or an innovator in the arts, may wish to bring about change in directions not before taken by the group. A radical rightist may work for an earlier belief, law, or practice.

Generally, the new dissenters work for change in new directions; for instance, the replacement of our corporate economy with a loose socialism, or the elimination of artistic censorship codes. They also want to go back to many of the psychological, economic and social arrangements of the past, based on a reading of that past which agrees with the conservative reading at many crucial points. Both see the free individual lost in urban dehumanization and bureaucratic government. Both look longingly back to a former life style which encouraged the "free" personality. The rightist sees the horseback hero and the pioneer farmer as central realities of this superior past. The leftist also glamorizes these hero figures, adding a third, the American Indian. The old expression "Be your own man," has its youthful counterpart in "Do your own thing."

Let two very different Americans dramatize this relationship: superstar and self-styled rightist, John Wayne; and black poet, playwright, militant LeRoi Jones (Imamo Ameer Baraka.) In the cover story of the August 8, 1969 issue of *Time Magazine,* John Wayne was officially sanctified as "the essential American soul," his worth finally being recognized in "the frontier town of Hollywood." In his early career, "the trick was to release the violence in neighborhood theatres," but until he made *Stagecoach* under John Ford, he hadn't

really earned his "head-'em-off-at-the-passport." *Time* notes
accurately that "the public pays to see the Wayne western as a
native morality play." The superstar is also the superamerican:
a founder of the Motion Picture Alliance for the Preservation
of American Ideals. Combining image and politics, Wayne
produced, directed and starred in *The Alamo*. He said that as
Davy Crockett he wanted "to remind people not only in
America but everywhere that there were once men and women
who had the guts to stand up for the things they believed."
Wayne considers the Alamo a metaphor for America:

> There was Mexicans and there was us, there was black and there
> was white. "They tell me everything isn't black and white,"
> complains Wayne. "Well, I say why the hell not?"

Recall the "traits" which Frederick Jackson Turner listed as
shaping the typical American through the frontier experience?
Coarseness, strength, practicality, inventiveness, materiality,
restlessness, and most important, dominant individualism. On
screen and off, Wayne seems to embody the conservative
Turner Thesis.

Yet, according to *Time Magazine,* the late Terry Robbins
of Students for a Democratic Society considered John Wayne
"terrific and total. He's tough, down to earth, and he says and
acts what he believes. He's completely straight and really
groovy. I mean, if they really want to make a movie about Che
Guevara, they ought to have John Wayne play him." (Robbins
and two companions were blown up shortly after this
statement by explosives they were compounding in a New
York City townhouse. The violence-oriented Weatherman
faction of Students for a Democratic Society went further
underground and became virtually inactive.) LeRoi Jones
would probably say that this fat cat Wayne was "togetha;" he
knew his name; he had "soul." The LeRoi Jones analysis of
present-day America parallels the John Wayne analysis. In
Dutchman, his most famous play, Jones juxtaposes Lula, a
neurotic white woman, and Clay, an uptight black man. As
they sit next to each other in a roaring Manhattan subway,

Lula derides Clay for wearing an ofay uniform:

> What've you got that jacket and tie on in all this heat
> for?....Boy, those narrow-shoulder clothes come from a tradi-
> tion you ought to feel oppressed by....What right do you have to
> be wearing a three-button suit and striped tie? Your grandfather
> was a slave, he didn't go to Harvard.

Through a series of taunts Lula incites Clay into throwing off
what she calls his "civilized veneer." Frightening and fascina-
ting her, Clay roars out his disdain for the button-down
world's refusal to admit that black and white, right and wrong
are simple forces locked in violent struggle. He becomes a
"man" again — and Lula stabs him to death. John Wayne says
we haven't the "guts" for it any more; Jones' character says
we're "bald-headed, four-eyed ofays popping their fingers...
and don't know yet what they're doing." American man has
become a cipher.

In 1963, LeRoi Jones published an anthology called *The
Moderns,* filled with young writers who have been rebelling
against the dehumanization and demasculinization of America.
At least half the stories were set either in the American West,
or were thematically impelled by frontier themes. In the
Introduction Jones claims, "There is an openness to the West,
to the non-urban that might lead a man to believe in some
kind of new construction." The West is the last non-urban
area, a constantly self-renewing frontier. Unable to believe in
modern America, the rebelling writer looks for new life in
what Jones calls "the non-urban landscape, [where] existentialism can be reduced or extended to a way of carrying a deer
back to a cabin." In this anthology such youthful anti-
establishment authors as William Eastlake, John Rechy,
Edward Dorn, Diane di Prima, Paul Metcalf, Douglas Woolf
and Jack Kerouac fictionalize the faith. Edward Dorn has
commented that "The American West is the place men of our
local civilization travel into in wide arcs to reconstruct the
present vision, the native version, of the Greek experience....
The American West, still in our time, has nothing to do with
industrialization." It would take too long to summarize the

stories these writers have contributed to this anthology, but they range from a parable about The Bomb, set in the desert, to a harrowing depiction of a young Indian avenging his race by murdering a white girl to whom he has just made love.

Many of these stories carry on the tradition of movement through the mythi and real West that literary critic Kingsley Widmer calls "the hobo style." Jack Kerouac was an early creator of dissenting hobo heroes, particularly in his novels *On the Road* and *The Dharma Bums*. His freeswinging prose has reminded some of Thomas Wolfe, a few of James Joyce, and many more of undisciplined rhetoric. In any case, it fit his major theme: the need to break away from stifling middleclass America, to assert a masculine, individual vitality in the open country. Kerouac's roads inevitably run west. In *Big Sur*, a later novel, he recorded his impressions while on the road thumbing a ride:

> Sleek long stationwagon after wagon comes sleering by smoothly, all colors of the rainbow...the husband is in the driver's seat with a long ridiculous vacationist hat with a long baseball visor making him look witless and idiot — Beside him sits wifey, the boss of America, wearing dark glasses and sneering, even if he wanted to pick me up or anybody up she wouldn't let him....There's no room anyway for a hitch hiker...here is ten thousand racks of drycleaned and perfectly pressed suits and dresses of all sizes for the family to look like millionaires every time they stop at a roadside dive....And if he thinks he wants to explore any of the silent secret roads of America it's no go.

Kerouac's hero characters seek the self-styled freedom to live as their natures require, and that means no racks of dry cleaned clothes suspended over the back seat, no sleek station wagons, and plenty of "silent secret roads." In the western context of Kerouac's vision, dissent means becoming a hobo again. In *The Literary Rebel*, Kingsley Widmer distinguishes the hobo, who works and wanders, from the tramp and bum, who seeks identity through inaction or alcohol. The hobo is attracted with sexual force to the open roads on which he travels west alone, or with male companions. Widmer believes that "individual male separateness" has been a crucial part of the hobo ethos.[3] This is true in Kerouac's novels; but the New Deal, and then the Second World War made hoboing harder. Prosperity, urban sprawl, welfare laws and social expectations caused Widmer to conclude, in 1964: "The truly distinctive hobo road exists no more, and with it goes part of the rebel's autonomous quality."

As Widmer was writing this, the counter culture was disproving him. A new kind of hobo was fashioning a new kind of rebellion, its roads leading west and its ethos grounded in western primitivism. At first, the hippies gathered in New York and the Bay Area to celebrate the hobo possibility. They collected in ghetto pads or "lodges," continuing the interest in Buddha, Jesus, Krishna and Asian life styles that had fascinated their beat predecessors a few years before. It looked as if they were new beats, for their gurus included Allen Ginsberg, Gary Snyder and Alan Watts, all saints of the earlier movement. In fact, the two movements, followed the same road. From the streets of San Francisco, the rebels spread along the roads of California, into the Sierras, down toward Los Angeles, over to the mountains and deserts of the Southwest, and particularly into Hopi and Navajo country. The interest of the earlier beats in the American Indian had been genuine but casual. The heroine of Kerouac's best novel, for example, was an American Indian, but her Indianness was not the prime feature of her consciousness. The hippies are the first group of Americans, excepting the Quakers and a very few Indian agents, capable of unpatronizing brotherhood with the Indian.

The hippie relationship with the American Indian is often considered superficial, and it is true that many Indians do not welcome it. Detractors point to whites wearing deerskin dress, bead necklaces and belts, constantly searching for peyote and mescaline, and aping the wigwam and the papoose. Actually, the western search being made by the hippie hobo for an Indian tradition is many-leveled and serious-minded. One indication is the contents of Haight-Ashbury's leading underground newspaper, *The Oracle.* During its two years, the paper

carried interviews, lectures, letters, articles and poems, advertisements, sketches, psychedelic illustrations, confessions and
recipes — in short, a thorough documentation of hippie life
style. *The Oracle* was in the lusty tradition of San Francisco
and western journalism. Nothing as inchoate, uninhibited and
intellectually innocent was published by similar groups elsewhere in the country. There were frequent sketches of
Amerind faces, or full bodies on horseback, sometimes in
praying position; Navajo blanket and amulet patterns; a variety
of dress, feathers, smoking campfires, peace pipes, axes and
other artifacts of Indian civilization. In a particular 1967
edition (otherwise undated) there is a full page of "Sioux
Songs." "Teonanacatl," a major article, emphasizes man's duty
to the supernatural commonly found in North American
Indian tradition and heightened by the use of "plant sources
of chemical energy." The twin interests in the spiritual and the
psychedelic are beat-hippie contributions to the new dissent.
Contrary to popular belief, the spiritual quest is primary. For
the most part, psychedelics are regarded as means to the
spiritual end. The spiritual quest is presented in lay scientific
terms in "The Hopi Life Plan," an interview with a Hopi
"messenger" recorded at Oraibi. The life plan is interpreted
from a petroglyph, reproduced in *The Oracle,* and it depicts
the origin of life, the path of life, and the journey of the first
men up from the underworld. Other figures represent the "last
great world war" when the pure ones will survive to renew the
species. An even more interpretive article, "Kiva," sketches a
"transcendent merger of Hindustani mysticism and Amerind
spirituality...seeming to make one vast Deccan [plateau] and
wide prairie, Himalayas and Rockies where races of men
assume a oneness as well." The writer proposes communal life
to achieve this blend, offering the Hopi kiva as a "matrix for
liberation," and "center for energy."

Indeed, an increasing number of new dissent whites seek
truth through such tribalism. Most of the white tepees are set
up in the West, where larger chunks of land with fewer
people nearby are available on less expensive leases. In its July

18th, 1969 issue, *Life Magazine* ran an article entitled "The Commune Comes To America." The commune had been in America for thousands of years, but the subtitle ignored history, proclaiming: "Youthful pioneers leave society to seek, from the land and one another, a new life." This "new life" is achieved by returning to the old life. The lead paragraph says: "Their hair and dress, their pioneer spirit, even their Indian tepees evoke the nation's frontier beginnings." While noting differences between these and native tribesmen (like affluence), *Life* presents the new dissenters in a continuing set of appropriate though overdone western images. By reducing their life style to the subsistance level, these new pioneers are deliberately returning to the individualism and especially the self-reliance of an earlier time. They understand what John Wayne is all about — to a point. Were he to mosey into their commune and settle down at their campfire, he would understand what they were all about — to a point. Everyone would agree that life in nature was more useful, honorable and manly than life in the urban world.

But at this point, their values would diverge: while the members of tribal communes are escaping affluence, John Wayne is basking in his millions, proud of the hard work by which he earned them, and damned if he wants to share them with bums, communists, queers or student radicals. In other words, the mythic West *looks* the same around that campfire, but it means practically the opposite in value terms. The individualism which the conservative and the new dissenter seek is similar in how it feels, in what it does for the spirit, and in the way it strengthens and harmonizes the parts of the body. At the level of what Walt Whitman called "personalism," it is the same; but when John Wayne extends his values, he envisions a world which the new dissenter rejects with horror. To Wayne, our collective middle-class defect is lack of true grit in violent competition for riches, fame and self-esteem; the new dissenter sees the same middle-class America being destroyed by an overdose of that very competitiveness and self-centeredness which Wayne finds lacking. Wayne would say, "Compete and fight, as men did in the old west." The new dissenter would say, "Stop competing, stop fighting, seek higher truths through the spirit, through a return to nature."

In these instances and many others, the West has become a battleground for the clash of prevailing culture and counter culture. At the same time, the vitality of western myth encourages a kind of lighthearted, escapist parody that is essential to a group that takes life very seriously. A well-made western like *Shane, Red River,* or *True Grit* is as popular among the new dissenters as it is among the mass of Americans whose life style they reject. *Time Magazine* reports that Abbie Hoffman, a yippie leader, likes Wayne's "wholeness, his style." *Time* dubs Wayne "one of the pop-artifacts of contemporary life," which is exactly why Abbie Hoffman delights in him. It is no longer possible to enjoy the plantation myth, the martial myth, or the myth of happy affluence. Killing under a cactus is entertaining, but not killing under a magnolia tree.

Another reason for the appeal of the West to the new dissenter is that the second and third largest color minorities are centered there. As both Mexican-Americans and Indians began to agitate for liberation, they made appealing brothers in commitment, especially for white dissenters who were uncomfortable with the more intense and dangerous alternatives of black militancy. It is probably true, though, that as this struggle has intensified, youth in the counter culture have found it less possible to watch John Wayne gallop across the screen shooting "Injuns."

A final reason for the importance of the West to the new dissent derives from all the rest, but is more than their sum: the West is believed even in the counter culture to be the most truly American part of America. Though Turner's chauvinism is not acceptable, his insistence on the centrality of the frontier in giving America shape, substance and texture makes as much sense to the counter culture as to the mainstream. Contrary to reports from the right, the new dissenters are not disloyal, unpatriotic or treasonous. With astonishing unanimity, they are American Utopians; they dream of a society which acts out the freedoms that western myth depicts as having been present in the old West. They believe that a moral West is still possible. Like San Francisco poet Lawrence Ferlinghetti, they are "waiting for the discovery of a new symbolic western frontier."

1. Joseph Campbell, *The Hero with A Thousand Faces,* Cleveland, 1956, pp. 19-20.

2. See Bronislaw Malinowski, "Myth in Primitive Psychology," in *Magic, Science and Religion,* New York, 1948.

3. Kingsley Widmer, *The Literary Rebel,* Carbondale, 1965, "The Hobo Style."

Conclusion: The West in the New American Consciousness

The preceding chapters have discussed the effects of commonly held western ideas on mass consciousness. As America's most formative myth-subject the West has altered the presumptions of Americans about their place in both the political world and the moral universe. The Old Western was, in the words of Leslie Fiedler, a "psychedelic necessity," blowing the minds and exciting with an almost sexual intensity the imaginations of Americans for more than a century. It was a compulsion that altered perceptions. It justified the behavior of an aggressive technological society. When embodied in such popular, and therefore consciousness-influencing works as Turner's Thesis, Teddy Roosevelt's *The Winning of the West*, George Stevens' movie version of *Shane*, or Sam Peckinpah's *The Wild Bunch*, its Contradicting Romances have taught that the middle-class community virtues could be achieved by lawlessness, violence and racism. The Romances encouraged the elimination of what Fiedler calls "the radically different other" — the Indian, the intellectual, religious or racial deviant, and later the hippie — but for the sake of society. In the Old Western, the Indian was the ultimate if not the always-seen enemy, the prime object of worthy hate and commendable violence. Only after his "removal" could the focus of negative attention shift to cattle barons, hired gunslingers, profiteering bankers or claim jumpers. In all cases, the Old Western glorified the imposition of a Lockian scheme of property, labor and law on a wilderness originally controlled by a people with an opposing scheme. Even more deeply than the Indian person, the enemy was the circular, communitarian and non-progressive Indian world view. Locke's *prima causa*, Reason, framed the Old Western: the Hero was always the most practical of men, always able to *function* to victory. We were to understand that the Western Hero had made possible the transformation of the new world of nature into fit property. The settlers may have organized the property; the Western Hero got them there in the first place.

But this Lockian vision of a new reality wore thin; gradually, as we have glimpsed in previous chapters, the relationship between enemy and hero began to change. The counter-culture expressed a growing skepticism that "property" was worth the criminality necessary to claim it. The enemy would become the hero, and the hero would often be the object of laughter, scorn, even hatred. In one stunning example, *Little Big Man,* Thomas Berger redefined the mythic West by reversing it. Jack Crabb was a hero by default, doomed — or destined — to lose even when he won. Survival was his victory, though after each scrape he had less. He lost two separate families, calling after calling, job after job, society after society. The ultimate default was that he alone survived the Battle of the Little Big Horn — but of course you aren't supposed to believe that, because as Berger himself has said of his technique, "the fiction is all, the invention, the lying." Custer and Wild Bill were preening egomaniacs and Kit Carson, a grubby, bandy-legged old sot. White women being raped by drunken Cheyenne put up no fuss. While being whipped by white technology and numbers, Indians continued to believe with Old Lodge Skins that they would have to rub out the yellow hairs, who "do not know the center of the world." Whereas the wilderness of Leatherstocking, the Wyoming of The Virginian, or the mountainous frontier of Shane had fit together with their calling, the West of Little Big Man was a roaring mass of incongruities made both mythic and believable by a new kind of western language combining the vernacular and the figurative. In the ultimate reversal, for the first time in a widely read work of fiction, Indians sounded, thought and acted like human beings. By 1968, Leslie Fiedler could say that all along the archetypical Western had been "a fiction dealing with the wilderness of a transplanted WASP and...an Indian."[1] Even as Shane rode the screens of America in 1954, culture critic Robert Warshow sensed the shifting western focus: "The truth is that the Westerner comes into the field of serious art only when his moral code, without ceasing to be compelling, is seen also as imperfect."[2]

So long as the human actualities of western settlement had been kept at a distance the West could satisfy the simple codes and surface relationships necessary in entertainment. This self-delusion required a continuing belief in myths impossible after the Second World War. The agonized reappraisal became national thought by 1955, the year that one critic has rightly called "the beginning of our own times." In San Francisco, Allen Ginsberg gave his first public performance of "Howl," and a few months later the City Lights edition of "Howl and Other Poems" went into circulation. This was also the year that Rock burst on America. Between the Beats and the new music, a counter-culture began to surface that would lead directly to the anti-politics of the Sixties, a widespread refusal to believe in our foreign policies, domestic programs, traditional leadership, customs — past.[3] Inevitably, the debunking of the past led to the central myth of the Western Hero and Western Settlement.

The Old West had to go. How could we believe in the right of anti-social gunslingers to shoot down opponents in town streets once we began to believe that America was an international gunman whose victims were crying out against her? Suddenly the violence we had digested like innocent candy bars became "real." The American West got mixed up in the American present, with the result that poets, novelists, historians, film makers and culture pundits began to conceptualize it as a complex part of a complex America, no longer a special symbolic reflection. While Hollywood ground out more third rate entertainment — proving once again American courage at the Alamo — in classrooms, libraries and a spreading assortment of imaginations the Alamo was being understood as American imperialism. While the Custer commerce continued in glossy local library editions, a swelling undercurrent of thought uncovered an eccentric tyrant who should have been drummed out of the Army.

Two major and overlapping Western Hero variations emerged from the chaos, the anti-hero and the outmoded hero. The anti-hero would be less than competent, would have lost the heroic code, would lack grace or chivalry. The outmoded hero would engage our sympathies as he fought for survival in the very society his earlier counterparts had scouted for, and would become the "radically alien other" that his Indian foes used to be.

The West in which both the anti-hero and the outmoded hero must function has also been radically changed. The storefronts and the dusty streets mean different things in the New Western, and the quality of life is questioned. A moral pall hangs in the big sky. The boulders, high forests, crackling deserts used to threaten whites because Indians knew how to ambush from them. Now there is an ambiguity about western nature created by white civilization itself. This interplay of new man and new landscape is crucial in E. L. Doctorow's 1960 novel *Welcome To Hard Times,* a parable about evil and good which explores the magnetism of violence, the inherent masochism of our fascination with the West. There is no hero. The narrator is the unofficial Mayor of Hard Times, a village squatting on a flat stretch of forbidding Plains near mining country. A plain man, the Mayor behaves neither as a coward nor a hero under fire. The story begins as a gigantic Bad Man from Bodie enters the town with no fanfare and simply takes it over, killing with random terribleness, maiming, raping, looting, burning and finally disappearing toward the mines. Out of this shambles the narrator-Mayor, a whore named Molly who managed to survive the Bad Man's terror, and the ten-year-old son of the first victim come together as a nuclear family. Along with an old Indian, Ben, they outlast the long winter while a new set of citizens emerges from the Plains.

But the psychological shadow of The Bad Man hovers over the rebuilt town, especially in Molly. She taunts the Mayor for not having been man enough to kill The Bad Man. She suffers from periodic delusions imagining his return. She trains the boy, Jimmy, to disdain the Mayor's weakness. Half believing Molly, the Mayor is dependent on his tormentor, and Molly needs the Mayor to hate while she tries to love.

They all know that The Bad Man will return as surely as the black clouds of oncoming winter. He is the nuclear reality of the West, a place unleashed upon time without order. The chaos has nothing to do with hostile Indians, the bloodshed is entirely white. The Bad Man is not simply a mean hired killer who wears gloves — the gunman in *Shane* — but anomie personified. He is not simply another Wild Bill, expert in arms if professionally above the law. Such men lived by a code, undertook and created ritual. They had a position at the edges of society. The Bad Man from Bodie is not a man at all, but a negative force-field of pure destructiveness without mind, personality or preference. By the time he returns, three seasons later, we realize that Molly has been waiting in fascination for her demon lover, has trained herself to enjoy being destroyed by him. So has the town, unprepared and open. As the Mayor-narrator says, "Of course now I put it down I can see that we were finished before we ever got started, our end was in our beginning." Then he asks the reader, "Do you think, mister, with all that settlement around that you're freer than me to make your fate?"

This moral connection is made inside the plot. On his return, The Bad Man is accompanied by miners. They descend on the town because the bonanza has given out and the author carefully sketches their rootlessness. Now The Bad Man's force-field includes a mass of ordinary men, plain enterprising Americans, the stuff of Mark Twain's Nevada, the salt of the Sweetwater mining communities. The riot that destroys Hard Times this second time is their collective contribution to society, the western barbarism stripped finally of romance, seen once and for all as Lawlessness. And the heroes of Democratic Settlement, the law-abiding pioneers, artisans, tradesmen and lawmen are also stripped of their myth-power. When Molly challenges Jenks, the town sheriff, to kill The Bad Man, the Mayor-narrator notes Jenks' "simpleton pride rising like manhood to her promises." Then he asks himself, "Or did he really believe he could stop the riot by killing Turner?" In either case, strength is illusion if not foolishness. What happens is that when Jenks pulls one of the saloon doors back he is blinded by the lights and The Bad Man easily pumps two shots into him. The men in the saloon scatter through the door, knocking the wounded Jenks off balance. Zar the saloon owner shouts "No, no," as Jenks fires, hitting him in the stomach. Jenks falls under a hail of fire.

There are no heroes in Hard Times because no one is equipped to conquer the malevolence of the violence inherent in western settlement. Finally, though, the Mayor unwinds barbed wire on the saloon porch, calls Turner, the Bad Man, out, wings him in the leg as he topples into the barbs, knocks him out and carries him like a gift to the family dugout where Molly waits. We might expect that after three years of torment this trophy would redeem the Mayor in Molly's eyes. Instead, she throws herself on the object she has psychologically longed to die by. The Bad Man reaches up and enfolds her just as Jimmy shotguns them both to death. The boy disappears then, riding hard on a mule and wagon, an adolescent replica of The Bad Man destined to turn up in some other western town. To complete the round of fated violence, the Mayor tells us that he is dying as he writes. The only person to survive in Hard Times will be the dead Swede's wife, who is insane. "But for Helga, I have the town to myself....The street is busy with the work of jackals and vultures, flies, bugs, mice. Together they make a hum of enterprise." Enterprising Lockian civilization has collapsed in a mad West.

There is only one Indian in the dead-end world of *Welcome To Hard Times,* and he lives right in town. But the changing vision of the Indian reaches into pulp fiction as well as into the specialized novel, and affects the image of the western landscape peddled to mass audiences. For example, the novel *A Death in Indian Wells*, published for newstand purchase in 1972, is set in another town in the open West. A garish cover shows three gun-wielding, mounted western hero types descending on a breech-clouted, tomahawk-carrying, feather-headed Indian. The author, Lewis B. Patten, is a Western Writers of America Spur Award Winner. In the manner of Louis L'Amour and Max Brand novels, *A Death in Indian Wells* has no style whatever. It is badly undescriptive, builds in no naturally rhythmic way, attempts to develop not a single interesting, much less complex character. The hero, sheriff Pete Handy, is a faintly smiling mouth and frequently narrowing eyes. The town of Indian Wells is presented with none of the atmospheric touches found in *The Ox-Bow Incident* or in *Welcome To Hard Times.* We are told that it lay in a valley below a marshy flat, that its earlier buildings had been of prairie sod, its later buildings of wood, that there were 117 residents and frequent buffalo-hunters, and that a tannery at the south end of town often bred an unbearable smell. To all intents and purposes, this is simply another example of commercialized western myth.

Yet the subtitle on the cover hints at something more: "COULD A SHERIFF WITH AN INDIAN SON STEM THE RISING TIDE OF BLOOD?" The hero is married and a father! What is more, his wife is a Cheyenne living out of town with her people, and their son Joseph, acting as Pete's deputy, is an Indian by the laws of racism. Gone is the asexual sheriff. Gone also is the aseptic anglo-western town sketched for the American reader as if all Indians sat patiently in *tepees* somewhere beyond the novel's horizons waiting for a Hollywood director to use them in a cavalry charge. Not only is the Sheriff's Deputy an Indian, but the Sheriff is known to love his Cheyenne wife. He had chosen to bring his son up in white society after the Sand Creek Massacre taught him the uselessness of trying to reconcile the races.

The precipitating situation tells us even more that the New Western influence has reached drug store book stands. Pete and his son are bringing in a drunken murderer. In conventional western fashion the author has them riding down main street. But then convention gives way: their attention is drawn to a crowd ogling something in the hardware store window — a young Cheyenne with a bleeding thigh wound and a frothing chest hole. Unconscious and close to death, he is chained to a ringbolt in the floor. Whoever had manacled him, wrist to ankle, had burned the flesh. The sheriff is outraged, his son infuriated. The townspeople look toward the son with racial hostility while the Sheriff finds out that three buffalo hunters had brought the young brave in, that the local blacksmith had made the manacles, and that the hardware store owner, Grosbeck, had agreed to display the brave because it would be good for business.

The terms of the ensuing conflict are far more complicated than the style of the novel would suggest. In places they achieve almost the level of tragedy. Inevitably, the Sheriff enrages the townspeople by insisting that the Indian is a human being. He forces the doctor to tend the dying brave, then arrests the buffalo hunters. The people expect that as an elected official Pete will do their bidding — but he does not. Justice requires that the dead Indian be returned to his people. When Joseph delivers the corpse, a powerful elder by the name of Badger encourages the suspicion that Joseph might himself have killed the young brave. Joseph realizes that he had been hoping all along to encourage a confrontation between Indians and whites. The townspeople had humiliated him and he half-hoped for vengeance through a raid on the town.

Tension mounts as Indians appear nearby. The Sheriff rides out to parley. Chief spokesman Spotted Horse demands the buffalo hunters as compensation for the corpse. Pete buys twenty-four hours of negotiating time and returns to town to find himself at dead center of his dilemma. As representative of the entire tradition of Anglo-Saxon law, he must insist that the buffalo-hunters be held for trial. The citizens want the buffalo-hunters given to the tribesmen to avoid the expected raid. From having lived much of his life as a white-Indian, Pete knows the Indian sense of justice demands that they deal with the murderers of one of their own. They do not comprehend what a white court of law is, and have no reason to credit white justice when an Indian is the victim. Curiously, both Indians and whites want the buffalo-hunters handed over, though for different reasons. And sense of duty must require the hero to reject both pressures.

The hours tick away and the dilemma becomes more viscous, until a new element is interjected: Pete's wife, Joseph's mother, walks alone across the no-man's land, feeling a compulsion to share her family's crisis. Her arrival precipitates an outcome filled with high dramatic irony, but flattened by lack of style. Pete puts his wife in the hotel, telling Joseph to visit her. Two hours later a delegation comes to the Sheriff's office demanding his resignation. Of course he refuses. He is given till midnight either to resign or turn the buffalo hunters over to the Indians. The townspeople's lever is Pete's family, now hostage in the hotel.

The situation forces Pete to confront those who had elected him at gunpoint in the hotel lobby, while a newspaperman he is protecting gets the room key, letting Joseph and his mother out. This is the first time the Sheriff has used force against his own constituency, rather than protecting their "interests," and he knows he is courting deadly resentment.

Ever since Joseph understood his motives, his conscience had been stricken. Now Joseph acts, knocking his father out and releasing the buffalo hunters. After tying them to his horse, he runs them over to the waiting Indians. This is clearly a sacrifice to protect the honor of his father by doing what his father needed to do, from all points of view, to stop the bloodshed — but could not do from a sense of duty. Irony closes around the solution. By bringing the hunters to his own people for justice, Joseph has removed the main reason the diehard few have used to instigate a raid on the town. By having lived with his father so long in a white town, Joseph has lost credibility. It is easy for Badger to inflame the others, accusing Joseph of being "one of them." Joseph draws in fury, Badger knifes him in "self-defense." In a final act of self-sacrifice for the general good, Joseph refuses to kill Badger with his drawn and cocked gun, realizing that Badger's death would cause the Indians to attack the town. As Joseph mounts, the knife in his chest, to ride toward Indian Wells, his own people puncture him with rifle shots. Joseph's ironic death removes his father's main reason for living a white life. The novel ends with Pete throwing his badge into the street and turning his horse toward the village of his wife.

A Death in Indian Wells reflects at the pulp level the new American consciousness, a reluctant racial fusion. More particularly it reflects the New Western, in which whites (the buffalo hunters and the townspeople) have become the villains while Indians (Joseph, Spotted Horse, Pete's wife, the manacled young brave, and the Indian community) have become the more functional representatives of justice. The central hero is still white, but Indian by adoption and preference. His values are grounded in Anglo-Teutonic world view, but he does not believe the white lives of the townspeople are more important or "valuable" than the red lives of the Cheyenne.

In the New Western, the white hero moves inevitably toward the Indian world. So does the Indian hero move toward the white. The structure of *Little Big Man* is built on this dual motion. In *Custer Died for Your Sins,* Indian critic Vine Deloria mentions three books which "give a good idea of the intangible sense of reality which pervades the Indian people." One of these is Berger's novel. Another is Hal Borland's *When the Legends Die,* in which a hostile Indian youth becomes a superb bronc buster, rises to fame and the fast life of the larger society, but finally returns to the Ute country of Western Colorado to find the age-old connections with nature that he had fled after his mother's death. The third novel, which Deloria claims to be the favorite of Indian people, is the less-known *Stay Away, Joe* by Dan Cushman of Montana. *When the Legends Die,* and F. Scott Momaday's

House Made of Dawn are "serious" artistic attempts to depict the impossibility of the Indian hero finding himself in the white world by shedding the self of the Indian world. Both seem to be saying that the worlds can never meet, that in some irreducible way they are blind to each other.

Stay Away, Joe says the same thing, but with broad, sometimes farcical humor. Those qualities which make it a favorite of Indians make it less "real" or compelling to non-Indians. It is difficult for non-Indians to relate politically to a work which pokes fun at nearly every one of its Indian characters. Where are the agonies of the oppressed? If one laughs too easily at the illogic by which Louis Champlain rationalizes the dishonesty of his son Big Joe, then one may be patronizing a primitive. Does one's amusement at Mama insisting on a porcelain toilet to impress white guests — when there is no running water in the house — smack of racism? The ethnic politics of the time would be better satisfied if Dan Cushman had projected a consistent image of Indians overwhelmed by white pressures, rather than Indians having a hell of a good time. They ought to appear tragically self-destructive (the manner of *House Made of Dawn*) or alienated (the manner of *When the Legends Die.*) But the unremitting joy of life that saturates *Stay Away, Joe* makes no apologies for Louis Champlain's foolishness, his son's rascality, their friends' violence, infidelity, drunkenness. Not a shred of "message" mars the vitality of this novel, a kind of reservation *Tom Jones,* and its lack of self-consciousness makes it the finest rendition of Indian world view so far published.

The plot is simple. Louis Champlain and his wife Annie, usually called Mama, live on a rundown spread in reservation Montana: rusted-out autos, collapsing corrals, a makeshift tepee for the ancient grandfather who bemoans the passing of old days and ways. A Congressman comes along to provide twenty cattle. Louis will be part of an experimental program for landless Indians. The Congressman believes he can get the necessary funds because Joe, Louis's son by an earlier marriage, is a Purple Heart World War Two and Korean War veteran. Along with 19 heifers and a young bull, Louis's friends arrive from all parts of the huge reservation — and eventually, the state. Louis is bound by custom to entertain them. Some pitch tents in his yard, some use their cars. He raids Annie's teapot for ten dollars for beer, then wins a horse race for fifty more. Fights, love-making, cooking and trips to Callahan's tavern for beer go on at the same time, and it becomes apparent to Louis that one of the heifers will have to be butchered for provender. In the midst of all this, Joe returns from Korea and the party picks up new momentum. The braggadocio son hands his father a fifty dollar bill for beer. When asked why he didn't return in the Cadillac he had written about, Joe casually remarks that he left it in the town of Havre.

When Louis wakes up at the end of the great bash, he discovers that his friends had somehow butchered the only bull instead of a heifer: the complication which organizes the rest of the plot. How can Louis replace the bull so as not to disgrace the trust of the Congressman? Joe promises to find a bull, taking more heifers as trade goods but using the proceeds for a long binge. While Mama accuses him of this treachery and Louis defends him, Joe makes love to Glenda, the tavern owner's wife.

Neither Louis nor Joe is disturbed by the passing of time, it has no literal meaning for them. Only Mama acts like a white, counting the hours, asking questions meant to probe Joe's literal intentions, and otherwise aggravating the situation by trying to organize it. Eventually an old bull is carted to the Champlain spread — but he spends all his time sleeping. Joe insists they be patient with the bull since he cost nothing. Louis's troubles multiply when Joe announces that he has made a deal to exchange two more heifers for a white-ribbon-winning young bull. Over Mama's objections Joe goes off only to return a few days later in new clothes, driving an emerald green Buick sedan — and without a bull. Like the jar on a Tennessee mountainside in Wallace Stevens' poem, the Buick takes dominion everywhere. It proves to Louis that his son really was a great rodeo-rider who overwhelmed them at Madison Square Garden; and to Grandpere, that Joe is a great chief. To Mama, this is the final irresponsibility — and she throws him out. After ruining his rims by riding on tires the jealous Callahan had flattened, Joe dismembers the Buick to buy drinks and grub. At this point Mama decides to make her house anglo middle-class, using the proceeds from two more heifers for new clothes, furniture, and a toilet. Joe and Mamie are shacking in the Buick when Glenda comes gunning for them in the presence of the visiting anglos. Soon all the cattle are somehow gone, Glenda runs off with another man, Joe and Mamie get married, and the new couple moves into the tavern with Callahan.

Where are redemption, lessons learned, disclosures of oppression, alienation? We are asked to take everyone's behavior at face value. This is not a tall tale, all the incidents are plausible, the outlook of each and every character is realistic. The only exaggerations are those of comic convention. The humor derives from world view. The Indians here are not able to cope with the kind of dollars-and-cents linear reality that shapes the dominant society around them. They are part of it — drive cars, handle money, trade cattle, get marriage licenses most of the time, overspend on time payments. In all these respects they share the culture with whites. But except for Mama and her daughter Mary, none of them attempts to become what the culture requires. Big Joe is in the grand tradition of the likeable rascal. It would be tempting to decide that he lacks morals, manners or scruples because his world has been ripped from its traditional moorings; but one of the greatnesses of the novel is that its central character demands acceptance entirely for himself. Whether white or Indian, now or a hundred years ago, in St. Louis or in a Yellowstone River valley village, Joe would be a rascal capable of great generosity but greater selfishness. His father is sketched in the equally cross-cultural tradition of the addle-headed, easy-going elder who will never succeed in life but will always enjoy it. Universally, his kind brings out the

nagging persistence of a Mama, bent on impossible respectability. Mama wants Grandpere to join the mid-Twentieth
Century long before the visit of high-class white folk prompts
her to pick-ax his tepee. She is angry with Joe because he
forecloses the respectability they might achieve through the
twenty cattle, not because he raises hell.

Critically, the problem of *Stay Away, Joe* is as persistent
as Mama herself. The hilarity, warmth and winningness of the
novel derive from the inability of its Indians to cope with
"reality." After accepting this at face value, the reader must
cope with the problem of stereotypes — and transcend it. A
novel which accepts its characters in their own right demands
as much of its readers. A whole new side of western writing
emerges with this unpretentious masterpiece. In the past it was
possible to live with and laugh at the absurdities of such whites
in the West as Mark Twain's acquaintances, or Cat Ballou's
friend Kid Shaleen. Since *Stay Away, Joe* it has become
possible to laugh at the absurdity of Indian life in the same
way, as part of the larger absurdity, not as racist patronization.

Looked at another and equally justified way, Big Joe is a
beleagured western hero asserting his individuality in the face
of systems which would dry up his natural animal appetite, his
need for the free life. He is a comic version of the Indian
cowboy, a frequent presence in the actual West. We shall never
know whether Joe rode broncs in Madison Square Garden, but
like everything else in his myth-creating behavior, there is
truth behind the lie. The Buick is one of his mounts, and later
he rides a Harley-Davidson motorcycle he gets by trading off
the Buick's transmission and cylinders. The hero wears many
guises in western myth, but Lawlessness is common to all of
them. Sometimes it is directed at upholding community, as
with Leatherstocking and Shane; sometimes at overriding
community, as with Wild Bill, Little Big Man and Butch
Cassidy. Big Joe carries the appeal of the second type to the
modern Indian world.

The importance of Big Joe for the New Western can be
better understood through his white brother in *One Flew Over*

the Cuckoo's Nest. Randle Patrick McMurphy is the perfect name to evoke the British Isles that gave us the township system, common law and the idea of a constitution. Brash, coarse, inventive, materialistic, impatient of abstractions, anti-intellectual, McMurphy comes close to a caricature of the ideal American frontiersman pictured by Frederick Jackson Turner. McMurphy might as well be an historical figure, he certainly is a mythic archetype. Consider his credentials. Refusing to play by society's rules, he overturns the psychological and political systems of Big Nurse's ward. He pretends to no superior ethic, fleeces his followers and enriches himself. Yet the result of this loving exploitation is their idolatry. He is the West's eternal poker player, speculator, fast buck artist, tall tale man, flimflammer, pimp: Little Big Man locked in a psycho ward. McMurphy is right off Mississippi riverboats, Virginia City streets. Taken literally or too seriously, he embodies the worst of the Old West. Big Nurse is right: society cannot afford him, and for its own survival has had to lock him out of it. Society is the Order necessary for permanent, ongoing civilization. Like Big Joe, McMurphy is an exotic social deviant reminding us of what we have surrendered in the name of The General Good: "How'd he manage to slip the collar?" the narrator, Chief Bromden asks himself. "Maybe he growed up so wild all over the country, batting around from one place to another, never around one town longer'n a few months...keeping on the move so much that the Combine never had a chance to get anything installed."

Tragically, McMurphy must destroy himself in order to be himself. And to destroy himself, he must save his fellow man. They are weak and lost, overwhelmed by Big Nurse and by the Combine she serves. McMurphy knows who he is, serves no one — but also knows the odds from the beginning. Bromden sees the nature of the tragedy. When toward the end, McMurphy crosses to Big Nurse's booth, crashes through the glass and tries to tear her apart, Chief tells us, "We couldn't stop him because we were the ones making him do it. It wasn't the nurse that was forcing him, it was our need that was making him push himself slowly from sitting—.'' Earlier, when McMurphy had begun to realize the power of the combine, the terrible odds against his gamble for life, he had tried to draw back from the challenge which the others relied on him to make for them. Their disappointment was a pressure he could not resist. To have refused it would have been cowardly and brutal. So, when Big Nurse "punished" the Ward for a minor rebellion by placing the tub room off limits to their daily card games, "one by one everybody else looked at him...faces turned to him, full of a naked, scared hope." Rising from the chair in which he had kept a hostile, pouty silence, McMurphy "walked with long steps, too long, and he had his thumbs hooked in his pockets again." Kesey heightens the moment with tall tale description: "The iron in his boot heels cracked lightning out of the tile. He was a logger again, the swaggering gambler, the big redheaded brawling Irishman, the cowboy out of the TV set walking down the middle of the street to meet a dare."

McMurphy the western hero in the modern world cannot win any more than Indian hero Crazy Horse could win in the West of one hundred years ago. But failure to resist would be admission that the free individual is less than the fettered whole. As with Crazy Horse, the physical resistance, the tactics in the ward, the psychological and body warfare, are extensions of a moral resistance necessary for all tragedy. McMurphy is wiped out, like Crazy Horse, and with a kind of knife. In modern America, the aseptic and incisive scalpel removes that part of the man which controls his will. He is lobotomized. The literary great grandson of Leatherstocking is destroyed by the very Order his forbears had destroyed the people of Crazy Horse for. As a New Western, this novel defines the 1960's. The madness and absurdity by which European and American existentialists had been describing their sense of the world since World War I achieves here its western apotheosis. The Ward is a western town and the only "sane" citizens are the inmates.

This is also a novel of the Sixties in that the Indian moves in reverse. At first a shock-treated, identityless vegetable, Chief Bromden pretends to be deaf and dumb. The model of the kind of white man who had destroyed the Chief's people now redeems him, shows him the way, so that "one night I was even able to see out the windows." Whereas Natty Bumppo had fastened the good Indian to his Order with chains of benevolent civilizing iron, McMurphy expiates that racial sin by helping the Chief free himself of the Ward. The Chief in turn "saves" McMurphy from a fate worse than death, life as a vegetable, by destroying McMurphy's body in an act resembling love: "The hard, big body had a tough grip on life...so much I finally had to lie full length on top of it and scissor the kicking legs." Chief Bromden escapes and the novel ends as he returns to his people.

The society that locked Randle Patrick McMurphy out of it was organized and ready to dispose of its free western men long before Big Nurse kept the schedules. In *Butch Cassidy and the Sundance Kid* the New Western locates the outmoded hero at the turn of the century. The final version of the movie script was dated July 15, 1968.[4] There is something appropriate about the arrival of this true cinema "western to end all westerns" on the cultural scene during the most traumatic, self-critical year America has survived in modern times. In addition to the assassination of two more national leaders, both mass heroes, 1968 saw the stormiest student unrest, with Columbia as the hurricane's eye. It was the year of the false "peace" as President Johnson announced a bombing halt and withdrew from politics. It witnessed the collapse of many old versions of the American Dream, while new values and behavior which had been confined to the radical fringes seeped toward the center. America would never be believed — nor believe in itself — the same way again. *Butch Cassidy and the Sundance Kid* played its part by dismantling the western expression of the old American Dream as if it were a precious antique. Its hero had never killed a man, was a poor gambler, and did not fight fair. His way of retaining leadership, when challenged at Hole-in-the-Wall by Logan was to deliver "the most aesthetically exquisite kick in the balls in the history of modern American cinema."

Butch is a *cinema* hero, a conscious artistic product practicing the now-sophisticated art of playing western hero. The piece of art, the "movie" was more devoted to its own perfection of tone, sound, tempo and myth-style than to serving either the commercial or, what is often the same, the emotional needs of its public for entertainment. So far does the script depart from tradition that there is no villain of the old order, no greedy banker, bought-out gunfighter, psychotic bandit leader. None of John Wayne's perennial foes appear. To the contrary, the villain is society itself, centered in a Superposse of relentless lawmen who track the heroes for a number of years, driving them out of the West, out of the United States and down to Bolivia. "Who *are* those guys?" Butch keeps asking. They are the killers of the western dream, a faceless collection of professional lawmen in the perpetual service of that arch-capitalist, the railroad tycoon. They are a law-machine for the larger technological mechanism of the railroad which nationalized the American economy, shaped the demographic patterns of half a nation; was the arteries and veins of that Enterprise which, in turn had always been the nucleus of The Dream. There is a direct historical line from John Locke to the Harrimans and all other railroad magnates. Expert railroad stick-up men, such as the Hole-in-the-Wall gang, were sufferable in newly settled lands. They could not be allowed in the efficient world of the Twentieth Century Limited.

Butch and Sundance are the last of the original issue in other ways. Here again we have the Male Companions, the American doubles of which Leslie Fielder and many other culture critics like to make much in Freudian terms. Butch the thinker, the mumbler, the nice guy. Sundance the doer, the cold, efficient, hard guy, a perfect blend of stoicism, strength and know-how — the White Indian. But because these are now-types, they have sexuality. The gorgeous schoolteacher Etta, who thinks of them both as "her men" (like Marian in

Shane) sleeps only with Sundance, the physical half of the splayed western hero. Etta is a "now" character too. She is the un-sentimental schoolteacher who makes up her mind to throw in with these outlaws because she's 26, single, "and except for being twenty-six and single and a librarian, that's the bottom of the pit." She is a kind of western radical chic (played appropriately by Katherine Ross, the actress who could handle The Graduate) not exactly hard, certainly not tough, yet not simply emotional. She does the job of being a woman as efficiently as Sundance handles his maleness. This is all believable because of the disconnection that continues between even the new western hero and the western woman. Butch and Sundance are still more into each other than either Etta or the outside world. Etta says, "all these years and we don't know each other at all," and she is right. As she leaves them forever they are watching a cinema version of themselves in a Bolivian tent theater. The audience is cheering the forces of order and jeering the Wild Bunch. Actors acting the actors who are acting the "real life" Butch, Sundance and Etta are mixed with images of the trio on the screen, a fiction inside a myth. Enthralled, the two men forget that Etta is about to fulfill an earlier pledge to darn their socks and patch their wounds, but never to watch them die. Having outlived their credibility as humans, they appear on the myth-making screen.

There is another twist. The impossible past is worth continuing to believe in, *so long as we do not also believe it to have been possible.* To achieve this paradox the line between fantasy and actuality is erased not only in the open-air theater sequence, but in the epigraph for the script where author William Goldman wrote, "Not that it matters, but what follows is true." It does not matter because if all that followed were an historical lie it would still be "true" in the collective consciousness. The New Western, then, is not so much asking us to disbelieve the old hero as to accept him in new terms. We do not have to give up the free western man. We have to find a new context for him. For example, in this movie we are no longer allowed to admire his capacity to kill. Butch has never killed a man till late in his Bolivian career. Even the arch-gunfighter Sundance, the ultimate marksman, never kills a character known to us as an individual. The two shoot down some soldiers in the final scene, and massacre a brace of bandits shortly before that. But nothing encourages the love of violence within us, there is no mythic permission for slaughter. The massacre sequence is anti-violence. A brief but deadly fussilade of fire is followed by another sound "as loud and just as terrifying...the loudest scream anyone ever heard," according to the directions in the scenario. The sound builds as the bandits collapse. When the screaming stops, the blood "continues to drain ceaselessly into the ground." Directions then read "Butch is shattered; Sundance is numb." This brief excursion into the American *cinema verite* obsession with spurting blood, cascading organs, lopped arms and slit throats really is a telling artistic refutation of the Romance of Lawlessness in that neither Western Hero has fulfilled himself by the bloodletting, both are emotionally shortcircuited by it, and both flee from its implications. Most significant of all, the composition of the film elegizes rather than eulogizes the violence.

No discussion of Butch and Sundance would be complete without the contratemps of *The Wild Bunch,* issued the same year. Its myth-figures are also out of step with their times. In the words of British critic Jim Kitses, The Wild Bunch represent "a way of life, a style of action, a *technology,* with no vision, no values, no goal." Their battle cry is "Let's go!" The question is where?[5] A lot of romantic rationalizing is current about the "new violence" in American films. One critic notes that when cinema directors expert in this art form have to choose between the "pathetic pods" of the general society and "a selfish outsider" they draw strength from the "corrupting but larger-than-life example."[6] A film like *The Wild Bunch* may reflect its creator's honest sense that violence is what human values are all about — at least this is what Sam Peckinpah and his sympathetic critics claim. But they are distorting the past, both the myth and the actuality, by disconnecting violence from the total of the western experience. In making it an end, toward which everything in the story is bent, these artists and critics create a separate value out of violence. If they believed with Genet in the redemptive quality of certain violence-expressions, one might argue with the correctness of their vision, but not with its integrity. The interminable slaughter of the Temperance Union marchers that begins *The Wild Bunch* is so much excess since it directly follows and leads back to a brutal scene in which children gleefully watch ants torture scorpions, a moment that leaves no doubt as to "message." *The Wild Bunch* is nothing more than an Old Western using certain techniques of art.

The outmoded heroes of both films must give way to the settled world in which criminality is syndicated rather than individual. But we are not asked to give the Western Hero up, not even in *Butch Cassidy and the Sundance Kid,* where we see many nonheroic sides to his code and his behavior. In their final moment the mortally wounded Butch and Sundance come careening like inevitable Western Heroes, guns ablaze, out the door to die under the concentrated gunfire of an enraged society — and the camera freezes them alive. There are many other affirmations. Sundance is as laconic as The Virginian, as superb a gambler as Wild Bill, as luminescently virile as Shane. In a famous poster, tapped from the still photos used in the New York City sequence of the film, Butch and Sundance are dressed as turn-of-the-century gentlemen. This is appropriate for both the traditional and the modern embodiments of the Western Hero. This "last gentleman" to use Robert Warshow's apt phrase, is seen still in "movies which...are probably the last art form in which the concept of honor still retains its strength."[7]

Butch Cassidy and the Sundance Kid is a serious work of art, and one of its objects is to honor this honor. But like the three musical interludes in the film, this honor will have an emotional connection with the situation, not a literal one. The myth has become fable. We know that surely, when the sight of Butch and Etta cycling around the pastoral countryside to

"Raindrops Keep Falling On My Head" seems not only acceptable in a Western, but appropriate. We must now feel that the Western Hero is not only historically impossible, but mythically impossible in the old terms. A new kind of central figure is taking shape here, capable of self-consciousness and aware of life's insoluble complexities.

This affirming motif runs through *Easy Rider,* released a few months after *Butch,* which takes another set of Western Heroes on a long journey backwards, if not into time then into attitude. Its reels run in mythic reverse as Wyatt and Billy move from west to east, finally to death in the myth-land of America's most violent inner self, the redneck South. *Easy Rider* is the formula un-western Western. Men dominate its landscape, women are strictly sexual and work objects. Horsepower substitutes for horses; the cycles mean more than humans can. Its heroes are anti-social, they live by breaking the law, they are fleeing the law; and to top it off, their sidekick is a *lawyer* who himself flees responsibility through booze and winning immaturity. Like a string of Western Heroes from Leatherstocking through Boone Caudill, the easy riders are fleeing the refinements and constrictions of civilization. Their goal, the New Orleans Mardi Gras, is itself a breaking of order.

Easy Rider updates the Contradicting Romances. Here at last we have them in their true complexity and mirroring the condition of American consciousness in the Sixties. Both Peter Fonda and Dennis Hopper spent much time, in the months after their film became the talk of America, trying to make the culture understand they had not created "heroes" as such, admirable dudes. Hopper told an interviewer, "Everybody seems confused about the end of the picture, and all I'm saying there is that we aren't very different from the two guys in the truck who shoot us."[8] Neither Wyatt nor Billy is a "nice guy" in the pre-1955 sense. Both struggle to free themselves of middle-classness, opposing the bigotry, corruption and "ugliness" of the great majority. Yet both behave with corruption and ugliness, if not bigotry. These variations on the Western Hero are not criminal — they are not The Bad Man, not even the Hole-in-the-wall Gang kind — yet they are clearly not virtuous. They are not The Good Man. They enact Lawlessness, but not as in the old pattern, to pave the way for or to protect Settlement. In *Easy Rider* we find the negative resolution of the Contradicting Romances. Wyatt and Billy go outside the Law to make a fortune — in order to free themselves. But we are given to understand that they must break out of society because the world built by Lockian values is corrupt. The violence they endure is laid on them by decent folk. The values of the society for which the old Western Hero cleared the West of the old western enemy, the Indian, have now proven themselves worthless. The anti-hero, or the old hero turned inside out, can only yearn to fulfill his larger-than-life mission by *opposing* community. The Romance of Lawlessness and the Romance of Democratic Settlement are reduced to ridicule. In their deaths, Wyatt, Billy and the charming lawyer George leave behind an empty West through which heroes without purpose or values ride, searching for impossible security and tradition which they feel compelled to reject upon contact. This is the poignancy of their encounters with the rancher's family, and then with the commune in New Mexico.

New Westerns such as *Easy Rider* and novels such as *Welcome To Hard Times* suggest that the American Dream is dying. Through their critical attitude and the art employed to project it, western American writing has joined the culture and will help us understand where we go from here. It may be that, as was discussed in previous chapters, the "new man" of our time will be a combination of old western freeness and a fresh commitment to the human heart. The most positive comment on *Easy Rider's* meaning was made by Dennis Hopper himself. "Don't be scared," he said, "go and try to change America."[9]

BIBLIOGRAPHY

Austin, Mary. *Earth Horizon.* New York. 1932.

Austin, Mary. *Lost Borders.* New York. 1909.

Berger, Thomas. *Little Big Man.* New York. 1964.

Billington, Ray. *The Far Western Frontier.* New York. 1956.

Bode, Carl. *The Anatomy of American Popular Culture.* Berkeley. 1959.

Calverton, V. F. *The Liberation of American Literature.* New York. 1932.

Campbell, Joseph. *The Hero with a Thousand Faces.* Cleveland. 1956.

Clark, Walter Van Tilburg. *The Ox-Bow Incident.* New York. 1943.

Coleman, Rufus. *Western Prose and Poetry.* New York. 1932.

Crane, Hart. *The Bridge. Collected Poems.* New York. 1933.

Croly, Herbert. *The Promise of American Life.* New York. 1964.

Curti, Merle. *Probing Our Past.* New York. 1955.

Dana, C. W. *The Great West.* Boston. 1856.

Davis, H. L. "Open Winter," in *Team Bells Woke Me and Other Stories.* New York. 1953.

DeVoto, Bernard. *Mark Twain's America.* Boston. 1932.

Doctorow, E. L. *Welcome To Hard Times.* New York. 1960.

Ferril, Thomas Hornsby. *Westering.* New Haven. 1934.

Fiedler, Leslie. *The Return of the Vanishing American.* New York. 1968.

Foerster, Norman. *The Reinterpretation of American Literature.* New York. 1959.

Gillis, William. *Gold Rush Days with Mark Twain.* New York. 1930.

Homsher, Lola. *South Pass, 1868.* Lincoln. 1960.

"John Wayne," *Time Magazine.* August 8, 1969.

Jones, LeRoi. *Dutchman* and *The Slave.* New York. 1964.

Jones, LeRoi. *The Moderns.* New York. 1963.

Kazin, Alfred. *On Native Grounds.* New York. 1942.

Kerouac, Jack. *Big Sur.* New York. 1962.

Kitses, Jim. *Horizons West.* Bloomington. 1969.

Kraus, Michael. *The Writing of American History.* Norman. 1953.

Locke, John. *Of Civil Government.* Chicago. 1966.

London, Jack. *The Call of the Wild.* New York. 1914.

151

London, Jack. *Martin Eden*. London, 1946.

London, Jack. *The Sea-Wolf*. New York. 1945.

Mack, Effie Mona. *Mark Twain in Nevada*. New York. 1947.

Malinowski, Bronislaw. *Magic, Science and Religion*. New York. 1948.

Manfred, Frederick. *Lord Grizzly*. New York. 1971.

Marx, Leo. "The Vernacular Mode in American Literature." In Joseph Kwiat and Mary Turpie, *Studies in American Culture*. Minneapolis. 1960.

McMurtrie, Douglas. *Pioneer Printing in Wyoming*. Cheyenne. 1933.

Minutes of the County Commissioners, Carter County, Territory of Dakota, 1868-1870. Western History Division, University of Wyoming Library.

Mott, Frank L. *American Journalism*. New York. 1941.

Mumford, Lewis. *The Golden Day*. New York. 1926.

Neihardt, John. *A Cycle of the West*. New York. 1949.

The Oracle. San Francisco. 1967 issues.

Pence, Mary Lou and Homsher, Lola, *The Ghost Towns of Wyoming*. New York. 1956.

Raymond, Rossiter. *Statistics of Mines and Mining*. House Executive Document No. 207. Washington. 1870.

Rourke, Constance. *American Humor*. New York. 1931.

Sandburg, Carl. *Slabs of the Sunburnt West*. New York. 1922.

Schaefer, Jack. *Monte Walsh*. New York. 1963.

Schaefer, Jack. *Shane*. New York. 1949.

Smith, Henry Nash. "The Feel of the Purposeful Earth: Mary Austin's Prophecy." *New Mexico Quarterly*. 1931.

Smith, Henry Nash. *Virgin Land*. New York. 1950.

Soule, George. *Encyclopedia of the Social Sciences*, Volume IV. New York. 1931.

The South Pass News. Western History Department. Denver Public Library.

Stone, Irving. *Sailor on Horseback*. Cambridge. 1938.

The Sweetwater Mines. Bancroft Library. Denver Public Library.

Taylor, Bayard. *Eldorado*. New York. 1850.

Turner, Frederick Jackson. *The Frontier in American History*. New York. 1920.

Twain, Mark. *Roughing It.* New York. 1872.

Warshow, Robert. *The Immediate Experience.* New York. 1962.

Whitman, Walt. *The Whitman Reader.* New York. 1955.

Widmer, Kingsley. *The Literary Rebel.* Carbondale. 1965.

Williams, John. "The 'Western': Definition of a Myth." *Southwest Review.* Fall, 1961.

Wright, Louis. *Culture on the Moving Frontier.* Bloomington. 1955.